OVERCOMING
CRISES

STRATEGIES FOR ADDRESSING, MANAGING AND RECOVERING FROM ANY CRISIS

DR. SAMUEL ODEKE, DSL

CONTENTS

ACKNOWLEDGMENT

There is no big undertaking that can happen single-handedly. Even though I authored the book and it has my name, I could not have accomplished all the work required without the contribution of some key people.

My family has always believed in me. They always bring me joy and remind me that I have an obligation to make a difference in the world.

My friends have always stood with me. They have given me feedback and inspiration. They have taught me some important lessons of my life and I carry these lessons with me everywhere I go. The lessons I learnt from my friends have been my classroom as I grow as a leader and become the leader God intended me to be. They have taught me that sometimes you win and sometimes you do not.

My editors took my raw and rough thoughts, reviewed all the materials and turned them into what you can use to safeguard and protect yourself from crises. There are also a number of wise, gifted and excellent mentors over the years that have always wanted the best from me. They keep mentoring and encouraging me to grow and achieve more.

All of these people taught me. I learnt a lot from them and keep learning. We learn until we leave the planet. So, I invite you to use the ideas in this book to your benefit and share with your family, friends, associates or your organization. As well, please share it with leaders at all levels.

FOREWORD

We live in troubled times! To mention just a few, from the Boko Haram insurgency in Nigeria, Cameroun, Chad axis in West Africa to the uprising and crises in Libya, Syrian, Egypt, Turkey, and Yemen which are exacerbated by the crisis of the gulf countries in the Middle East. So also, from the hurricanes and wild fires in America to the earthquakes on Iran-Iraq border and North Korea. We witness violence and terror attacks of innocent people in United States, Egypt, Kenya and Somalia among many nations. In a world that is caught up in these natural and man-made disasters, the unpredictable nature of these conflicts and crises overwhelm victims, governments and the international community, especially as valuable human lives, livelihoods, and property are destroyed. It is true that in many instances, humanitarian organizations, governments, and the international community provide relief materials, which give some level of respite but recent field research and interactions with refugees, internally displaced persons, social workers and the humanitarian community reveal that recovery from distress take more than just food and non-food items.

To recover from crisis, it takes a conscious effort by all – including victims of distress - to plan and implement such strategies accordingly and Dr. Odeke attempts to enumerate these strategies in Overcoming Crisis. The book carefully highlights the power of integration, leadership and management of crises and takes us on a journey on practical ways of overcoming crisis. Additionally, rather that resign to fate as most victims of crisis do, the book makes us to realize that distressed times are not times for stagnation, but times for self-discovery, growth, and development.

Overcoming Crisis is a book for everyone! I therefore recommend it to people of all occupations, including social workers, leaders, institutions, government and the global humanitarian community.

Dr. Titus Terseer Orngu
Gender Technical Advisor
United Nations Women Organization
North East Nigeria

DEDICATION

The book is dedicated to the only True and Eternal God, the Alpha and Omega. I believe that God Who created everything also allows crises to come into our lives so we can be closer to Him. God creates seasons. Seasons are an indicator that nothing on earth is permanent. A change in seasons is a signal that change is on the way. Get ready for change. Get ready for a new season. Get ready for a crisis!

This book is also specially dedicated to the 7.5 billion people in the world. Everyone alive today will experience a crisis at a certain point in his/her lifetime. The book offers strategies for managing and overcoming any crisis. Acquiring knowledge and understanding will equip any person with a more effective way to respond to crises, rather than react to events or circumstances which he has no direct control over.

Caution: Do not become a victim of crises. Get ideas, learn concepts, and practice what you learn in this book!

A LOOK ON THE INSIDE

Over many years, I have had the privilege of working with large humanitarian organizations including the United Nations (UN). Working for those organizations has meant so many things to me. Especially, I call to mind the interactions with a variety of people, leaders in diverse settings, work environments and places. I have served and worked with excellent managers, supervisors and leaders. I have also worked in many nations of the world in addition to Uganda.

Through those interactions and working opportunities, I noticed that some people had the resilience to handle crises while others were completely subdued by sudden or unexpected events. I recall an experience in which a supervisor wept as a result of hearing the news of the sudden loss of a family member and guardian to Ebola. I recall another event in which a terrorist attack left a group of us in shock and terrified after several colleagues were killed. I watched both men and women go through the most difficult and life-changing experiences.

What was most interesting to me is that I saw the human spirit and the Holy Spirit at work during those challenging periods. Some of the people were able to learn the most valuable lessons from the pain and stormy experiences they went through. I do not know whether any of their families, friends or associates possess the depth of wisdom that those individuals possess. Though I have not asked anyone of those people to write their stories, I hope to do that someday. I believe those stories will be eye-opening to the fact that a crisis can actually affect anyone.

I recall travelling one night to the Entebbe International Airport, Uganda, with my wife. We parted amid hugs and she drove towards our home in Kampala. However, as she was crossing the humps on her way home, a speeding vehicle rammed into her own vehicle from behind. Moments later, she called to tell me that she had gotten in an accident. For the next couple of days, she was in a hospital nursing injuries from the accident and enduring even more pain.

How do you deal with pain when a crisis hits you? How do you deal with a plane crash that kills both your parents? I had a close friend whose cousin was diagnosed with cancer. He was progressive, developmental and a public servant. He had a wonderful family. He had resources and money. He got the best treatment from India. Nevertheless, when the cancer could not be treated anymore, he left his wonderful wife and kids behind. How do you deal with such an experience? I had a similar experience when I lost my mother and father suddenly without having any indication that they would pass on. It was a shock. It was unexpected event. How did I overcome? This book contains some of the lessons I learned as I ventured to deal with my personal crisis.

In the next edition of this book, I will include the stories of the people who have endured the most challenging moments of life and how they overcame the crises. In this edition, however, each of the chapters is packed with information that is useful for your growth and survival from crises. Even if you consider yourself a fine leader or smart person, crises will always have an impact on you. I have come to the conclusion that a crisis can either be an opportunity or a tragedy, depending on how you approach it. Overcoming a crisis, however, is critical so that you benefit from the impact it brings with it. What is my recommendation? Read this book carefully. Take notes. It will inspire you and prepare you to face any painful experiences and situations in your lifetime.

PREFACE

What will you do when you are hit by a crisis? Does a crisis affect you alone every time? No! It affects everybody in the world. Nobody is immune to crisis. No corporation or nation is immune to crisis. If you have not encountered a crisis yet, be sure it is on the way; it will arrive soon or later. When there is a crisis, followers often look toward the leaders. Leaders also look at stronger leaders for ways to tackle local, regional or international crises.

What do you do when the unexpected happens? What do you do when a natural calamity hits you or your community? What happens when things change unexpectedly? What happens when your spouse dies or decides to file for a divorce? What happens when you have your assets foreclosed by the bank due to your deepening financial crisis? What do you do when you are informed your current contract will only be extended for three or four more months and after that, you are out of job? What do you do when your son announces he is a gay? What do you do when the family member you cherish crashes in a car accident? What about when your spouse dies in a plane crash? What about when your house is demolished by the city's authorities for a violation of some sort? Or, when the court demands that you share your properties and assets with your spouse as a result of divorce? What about when your daughter gets pregnant? Or, when your investments are seized by government authorities? How do you deal with a hurricane or abrupt flooding?

The list of questions continues! How do you prepare to mitigate the adverse effects of a crisis? How do you leverage a crisis as an opportunity for progress or redress? How do you recover from a crisis? How do you handle a job loss? How do you survive when your trusted friends refuse to associate with you going forward? How do you cope with the grave sickness affecting your only child? What do you do when everything that you trusted – like friends, income, jobs or churches – changes? How do you deal with difficult times? How do remain stable in the midst of chaos, confusion or conflict?

When a sudden change occurs, a crisis can kick in. Many people never think of a crisis until it happens. Too often, people think they are immune. I have met people who think they own the universe. These people speak with arrogance that some crises are for other people and can never happen to them. I believe every person will experience a situation for which he or she was not responsible. In fact, you will experience circumstances which you cannot stop or control. This is what we call a crisis. It could be a marital crisis. It could be a financial crisis. It could be a leadership crisis. A crisis most often happens unexpectedly. It is sometimes unpreventable but always requires management. You may be emerging from the death of a parent, loss of a job or loss of a business. All of these can be considered crises.

I have come to accept two important ideas. In life, expect things to change, creating unexpected results. Always prepare for the worst and the unseen. That is just how life on earth is. However, the tragedy is that many people do not have strategies, resources or ideas on how to manage in times of crisis. To manage a crisis, you need tools to help you manage the unexpected. You need information and knowledge. Most importantly, you need wisdom, which is specifically applicable to your circumstances. I am convinced that every human being will experience crisis, change and turmoil. This book is written to offer you tools for managing in times of crisis. I mean: any crisis. Crisis should be viewed as a benefit and an advantage.

During a crisis, there are people who benefit, and there are those who lose. Crisis affects children, families, organization and nations. Nobody is immune to the negative effects of crises except those who have ideas on how to manage it. This book is about how to prepare for, manage and overcome crises of any kind.

If you are a true leader, you need to build your knowledge base on how you can help your group of followers who believe in you to overcome a crisis. Everybody is a leader. Be it a father or mother. You have people that you influence. For instance, you influence and impact your family. Leaders always emerge when there is a crisis. So get ready to lead and learn how you can empower the people to survive a crisis.

INTRODUCTION

"Failing to prepare is preparing to fail."
~ John Robert Wooden

Crisis Affects Every One and The Whole World

Is there any corner of the world where there is no crisis? I believe every part of the world is facing some form of crisis and it is not known whether or when the crises will ever come to an end. Think about it. Our leaders are bewildered and perplexed. Our leaders are confused and make poor judgement in every decision. The so-called advisors are giving misleading strategies and solutions to emerging crises. There are several causes, which include globalization, information exchange and improved communication media. Events or developments that happen in any part of the world e.g., China, Cuba or Russia are heard about everywhere else in the world almost as quickly as it happened in the originating country.

Globalization as we know today has directly or indirectly caused governments to have limited control over their own borders. The Internet and social media networks facilitate the exchange of goods and services around the world. Global communication has been simplified with the advent of social networks, accessible radios, televisions and mobile telephones. The rate of advancement in technology is faster and no singular country in the world will ever be able to control the pace and rate of change. This alone is a crisis that will impact thousands of people.

Let me point you to the areas where change hits people the most. I believe the areas where change affects people are social, economical, political, psychological, technological, and cultural. Take, for example, cultural change. This could be culture shock as a result of inter-tribal or inter-ethnic marriages, differences in language or even communication challenges. These changes will impact generations.

Conflicts have emerged because of religious differences between Muslims and Christians, Hindus and Buddhists, to mention a few. Wars have displaced millions of people from their homes to camps. Global crises have affected people's lifestyles and cultures. Refugees have increased in the last decade with giant economies such as Germany adopting unacceptable values and principles to close its borders to those fleeing from war zones and crossing into their territory.

Also, technology, especially computers and cyber space, has totally changed the way life is lived in every corner of the world.

In schools and public transportation vehicles, you may have observed young people who are addicted to the use of various computer applications and social media platforms. I am not sure these young people are remotely aware of a looming crisis. There is a likelihood that a crisis will affect these young people and they are not aware of when it will occur. When a crisis hits the people or government, there is no control over it, but most importantly, it causes people to lose their livelihoods, business, jobs or streams of income.

In my country, Uganda, more than 90 percent of the over 40 million citizens are employed in the agricultural and private sector. The remaining 10 percent are in government. If the country experiences massive rainfall, it will cause displacement, including the destruction of some major roads. On the other hand, if there is a delay in rainfall, a drought will be experienced – leading to loss of jobs, income opportunities, food shortages and high rates of school dropout, prostitution and high levels of criminal activities, among other negative coping mechanisms. This is not unique to Uganda, but is what obtains in many countries in Africa and other parts of the world. The people who depend mainly on Agriculture for survival will directly be affected and experience a shock. They will experience a crisis.

Now, you may be wondering whether the 10 percent in the government sector will be impacted by such a crisis. Those who are employed in the private sector and in government are not immune to crisis. When prices of imports double and exchange rates increase more than was anticipated, business owners will start to experience the impact. The central banks will try to control the central bank rates and influence commercial lending rates to what is considered acceptable.

If one nation is affected by a crisis, not only will the citizens of that nation will be affected, but also will the neighboring countries. When war broke out in South Sudan in December 2013, other countries in the region – Uganda, Kenya, Tanzania, Ethiopia and Rwanda – were not spared. In Kenya, when conflict broke out after the disputed elections of December 2007, Uganda, South Sudan and Rwanda were all impacted. Uganda was affected by the influx of refugees, which incited a crisis. Over 1,200 people lost their lives, which was a national crisis affecting the nation at the macro level. At the micro level, families were affected by disintegration, separation, stress and social and economic problems. In countries such as Syria, Iraq and Afghanistan, the crises are affecting the people in the entire region. What happens in one part affects the neighboring states.

In what other ways do crises affect humanity? I believe several factors such as migration, international trade, trade policies and poor decisions are the cause of global crisis. When a crisis hits, even the rich business professionals will be affected and will not be able to stop it. Consider the terrorists attacking a bus park, killing and injuring several travelers. This will create a crisis. The threat of terrorism is present in every state, including powerful nations such as the United States, United Kingdom, China or France.

There is another angle to crises which is merely a dictate of nature. The forces of nature are unstoppable and uncontrollable. They often cause landslides, earthquakes, droughts, cyclones, floods, and famine. Every person will experience or encounter a crisis. In Asian countries, tsunamis are a common occurrence that affect millions of people. Many people get killed and the properties, assets and livelihood of people are destroyed. The major result of crisis is vulnerability and exposure to risks such as diseases and even death. It also causes people or leaders to panic, leaving people feeling frightened and with a loss of confidence in their leaders. Crises also cause disruptions in trade activities where buyers stop buying goods and services and sellers stop selling.

When a person owns a corporation or a company, it could be liquidated. A person who runs a church ministry might be forced out of office because of a character defect. A chief executive officer might be forced out because of a corruption scandal. The loss of a job or divorce is a crisis. Further, when things start to overwhelm you, they become a crisis. Take, for example, a health problem that requires you to change a lifestyle. You might be having a good time right now, but you need to understand the fact that things will change and it will affect you. How prepared are you? Are you ready to face the crisis? Are you capable of dealing with it?

If you have no or even some idea about crisis management, then this book is for you. The book exposes you to ways of dealing with and managing a crisis. It will also help you to thrive above any crisis. It requires that you master, as well as apply, those concepts and ideas contained therein. I also believe that you need to expose your family, friends, church and organization to the concepts contained in this book. The only group of people who survive and emerge from a crisis are those who have the insight, wisdom and knowledge of how to.

The greatest leader in time and out of time, Jesus Christ, had the following teaching for His trainee leaders, the disciples:

"Do you now believe?" Jesus replied. "A time is coming and in fact has come when you will be scattered, each to your own home. You will leave me all alone. Yet I am not alone, for my Father is with me. I have told you these things, so that in me you may have peace. In this world, you will have trouble. But take heart! I have overcome the world. (John 16:31-33)

This message is about crisis. It is about bad times ahead. Jesus is talking about His team getting scattered and he being left alone. Nevertheless, He comforts himself in the fact that He is with His Father. Jesus informed the disciples about the need to have faith and to know that a time will come when the group would be scattered. When things are scattered, what does that mean? It means things are falling apart or disintegrating. Disintegration can affect children, families, friends, groups, associations, organizations, communities or states. The interesting part is that Jesus mentioned these things. He mentioned the bad news about crises so that his followers would have peace in spite of any crisis they may encounter.

Wait a minute here. How can you talk about getting scattered? He also said that in this world, the disciples would have many troubles. Nobody likes trouble. People dread trouble. People fear problems.

Humans by design expect only good things. If you tell your family that trouble is coming, what will you observe? Fear, stress, anxiety and many other negative emotions. Suppose your employer tells you that you are losing your post in the next 2 months. Or, your physician or personal doctor tells you that you have a tumor or cancer. How will you respond? Are you prepared for trouble? Are you prepared for the unexpected? Are you prepared for disaster? How ready are you? Your level of readiness and awareness will enable you to experience peace, enjoy the benefits of crisis and maximize the opportunities that come along with it. What then do you need to do when your company falls apart? What about your nation? What do you do when the unexpected hits you? These are the reasons you need to read this book.

Joseph and the Famine Crisis in Egypt

There was no food, however, in the whole region because the famine was severe; both Egypt and Canaan wasted away because of the famine. Joseph collected all the money that was to be found in Egypt and Canaan in payment for the grain they were buying, and he brought it to Pharaoh's palace. When the money of the people of Egypt and Canaan was gone, all Egypt came to Joseph and said, "Give us food. Why should we die before your eyes? Our money is all gone." "Then bring your livestock," said Joseph. "I will sell you food in exchange for your livestock, since your money is gone." So they brought their livestock to Joseph, and he gave them food in exchange for their horses, their sheep and goats, their cattle and donkeys. And he brought them through that year with food in exchange for all their livestock. When that year was over, they came to him the following year and said,

"We cannot hide from our lord the fact that since our money is gone and our livestock belongs to you, there is nothing left for our lord except our bodies and our land. Why should we perish before your eyes — we and our land as well? Buy us and our land in exchange for food, and we with our land will be in bondage to Pharaoh. Give us seed so that we may live and not die, and that the land may not become desolate." So Joseph bought all the land in Egypt for Pharaoh. The Egyptians, one and all, sold their fields, because the famine was too severe for them. The land became Pharaoh's, and Joseph reduced the people to servitude, from one end of Egypt to the other. (Genesis 47: 13- 20)*

What does the absence of food mean? It means people are not having sufficient meals. Famine is a crisis. In times of famine, water becomes a huge issue. Food becomes a big problem. Any household, group of people or community that lacks food will be in crisis due to hunger. In such households or communities, many issues might arise. For instance, women can engage in negative coping strategies. They might engage in prostitution in order to survive. They sell their bodies in order to get what to eat for the day. They are forced to engage in those acts because they might not have alternatives. They do what is nasty with their bodies, often leaving them feeling depressed, unhappy and miserable.

Likewise, for young or older men, they engage in robbery or other criminal activities. Some might end up in jail or even killed. They become slaves to acts that are publically unacceptable. Women may end up getting infected with HIV or other sexually transmitted infections. The other consequences include loss of moral values and ethics, broken relationships and families or unwanted children.

The Value of Life

It is my conviction that there is nothing more valuable than human life. The life of every person on Earth has value. Nobody can replace or give back someone's life if it is lost. But gold, oil, diamonds, silver or money can be replaced or returned. It can be given back. A crisis comes to take away the peace, happiness and joy of people, families, communities and even nations. When all peace is lost, happiness is not seen and the joy of living is absent. Individuals, people and families will worry about the lack of food, clothes, accommodation and many other necessities of life. When the necessities for life are not available, worry sets in and affects people.

The leader of all time, Jesus Christ, counseled the people, especially the disciples who followed him. He said, "Do not worry about life." He told them not to worry about food, drinks or clothes. Why? Because that is not the most important thing. He said life was more important than any of those things. Matthew wrote the following words:

Therefore I tell you, do not worry about your life, what you will eat or drink; or about your body, what you will wear. Is not life more than food, and the body more than clothes? Look at the birds of the air; they do not sow or reap or store away in barns, and yet your heavenly Father feeds them. Are you not much more valuable than they? Can any one of you by worrying add a single hour to your life"? "And why do you worry about clothes? See how the flowers of the field grow. They do not labor or spin. Yet I tell you that not even Solomon in all his splendor was dressed like one of these. If that is how God clothes the grass of the field, which is here today and tomorrow is thrown into the fire, will he not much more clothe you—you of little faith? So do not worry, saying, 'What shall we eat?' or 'What shall we drink?' or 'What shall we wear?' For the pagans run after all these things, and your heavenly Father knows that you need them. But seek first his kingdom and his righteousness, and all these things will be given to you as well. Therefore, do not worry about tomorrow, for tomorrow will worry about itself. Each day has enough trouble of its own. (Matthew 6: 25-35)

Jesus said in clear terms. He said never worry about food, clothes or drinks. Whenever a person worries, it is an indication he cannot or is not doing anything to change the situation. Instead, he starts to panic or procrastinate. He starts to blame the situations around him. He never takes any action. The panic will even bring more problems than solutions. A person or a leader who worries does not have power to add to or increase his or her days of life.

In times of crisis, the solution lies in seeking God's kingdom. Seeking means to search the mind of God. Seeking means to be in right standing and relationship with God. It means to obey God and His word. Why should you do this? When God speaks, His Word can change the circumstances that have caused you to worry, wail or weep. Seeking God will cause the release of the things that you need: like clothes, food, drinks and a better life. Jesus commands us to seek the Kingdom of God and all the things that we need will be added or given to us. God knows what we need. God also knows what we do not need. If God gave us what we do not need, we will waste or mismanage it.

Let me give you an example: Suppose you asked God for a Land Cruiser and God gave you an airplane, would you be able to manage the airplane? Suppose you asked God for a house with two bedrooms, and God gave you a house with 25 bedrooms. What would you do with the rest of the rooms? Suppose you asked God for a job that pays $3,000 and God gave you one that pays a million dollars. What would you do with that money? I believe you might not be ready to manage and handle such responsibility.

In times of crisis, we must be realistic. Realistic means not to be idealistic. I have had the opportunity to watch leaders paid hefty salaries who ended up spending it on the alcohol that eventually killed them. I recall a colleague whom I worked with in a large humanitarian organization. This person was humble. He retired from work and received a huge sum in retirement benefits. Do you know what happened to him? He used the money to drink until he destroyed himself. He died due to heavy drinking. This was a result of carelessness and irresponsibility.

Are you responsible? To what degree are you responsible with the resources given to you by God? The person who passed on prayed to God for a job and God answered his prayer by giving him a job. After retirement, instead of using the resources that God gave him to make a difference (for example, build a grinding machine for widows), he wasted the money engaging in what I consider a careless act. He is not different from the prostitutes or criminal gangs who mismanage their bodies or expose themselves to hazards or risks. He, too, exposed his life to alcohol and he lost it.

Chapter One

WHAT IS A CRISIS?

"The Chinese use two brush strokes to write the word 'crisis.'
One brush stroke stands for danger; the other for opportunity In a
crisis, be aware of the danger - but recognize the opportunity."
~ John F. Kennedy

Understanding the Concept of Crisis

As we proceed, let us consider the concept of crisis. A crisis is something that happens which you have no control over. It affects you directly or indirectly. It can be an attack. It affects your environment. You have no direct role, responsibility and control. It is beyond your capacity. A crisis is also defined as an unexpected experience or unplanned event that affects you, your family, friends and communities among others. A crisis does not respect families, firms, governments or nations. A crisis is the change that occurs unexpectedly in life. A crisis can be brought about by a change in seasons. A crisis is a time when there is turmoil or uncertainty. During a turmoil, there is disturbance, confusion and uproar. There can also be commotion, disorder, confusion, chaos and instability. A crisis often causes these events among people, organizations including nations or states.

A crisis is something that happens which you have no control over. It affects you directly or indirectly.

No person, nation or region is immune to crisis. Every person, including powerful leaders, will experience a crisis at one point or another. I recall reading an article about the late powerful leader of Venezuela, Hugo Chavez. With all the power he accumulated including having a powerful army, he could not deal with a certain crisis. He lost his life to cancer. I also recall the former Ethiopian Prime Minister and freedom fighter, Meles Zenawi, who lost his life. These leaders were dealing with unexpected events. I believe these leaders had all the resources needed to deal with their health challenges but were unable to and ended up losing their lives. They were unable to overcome personal crises. The health problems may have started small and then became larger, more abnormal problems, which led to pathological problems that created a crisis.

In South Africa, President Jacob Zuma has been in the news for his struggle to keep political power. That is already a sign of a crisis. The leader of the largest African Nation, President Muhammadu Buhari, was for a long time in London for treatment of an unknown and undisclosed medical condition. This sounds like he is going through a health crisis. Back home in Nigeria, the citizens were worried. What do you call that? President Muhammadu Buhari has the opportunity to get the best treatment, even more so than the common people do. A crisis does not respect anyone. It does not discriminate. It affects everybody, any place or even nations.

In Uganda, Crane Bank in November 2016 was almost closed by the Central Bank of Uganda. The owner of Crane Bank is Sudhir Rupereila, who is regarded as the richest or wealthiest businessman in the country. He is an investor with many properties and assets. But, as you might imagine, the Uganda Central Bank had to take over the management of Crane Bank and also obtained bailout assistance from the government. How could this happen with all the wealth the businessman owns? A crisis affects everyone or any organization. Nobody is immune. No organization or business entity is immune. The examples above are just a few. Look around your community or village and you will see what type of crises is affecting people, families or communities.

Personal and Global Crises

What makes a crisis? How worse can the situation be? Have you had a crisis? Have you gone through a crisis? Is there a crisis right now in your corporate organization or family? These are important questions. There is no doubt that one person's crisis might be another person's opportunity. Moreover, a crisis is something that happens and humans have limited capacity to stop, avoid, postpone or control. Look at the global crisis caused by the recession in 2008.

The G8 nations were unable to stop it immediately. The crisis also affected the five permanent members of the United Nations. The five permanent members are USA, France, China, Russia, and Britain. Another term used interchangeably with crisis is disaster. How does a disaster occur? What happens when a disaster hits? What are the different types of disasters have you experienced in your life, firm, family or nation? Do you know people who have been through a crisis? Let us examine how crises happen and affect people, governments and world at large.

Broad Categories of Crises

There are two broad categories of crises: slow-onset and sudden-onset.

A Slow-onset Crisis

This type of crisis comes slowly. There are several examples of slow-onset crises. For example, you eat uncontrollably and gain excessive weight. Then one day, you notice you have back pains and breathing problems. You run to the doctor and the doctor decides to carry out various tests. The test results come back with the following findings: high blood pressure, high cholesterol, obesity and low ability to navigate and concentrate. Then the physician drops guidelines and instructions on how you are supposed to stop eating red meat, reduce salt intake, eliminate alcohol and reduce sugar intake. The doctor tells you that you must stop ingesting milk and bread. The doctor says, if you do not stop, the consequences of high blood pressure alone are higher chance of heart attack, brain damage known as stroke and kidney failure. What are you going to do about this? This becomes a crisis because suddenly you need to change your lifestyle. Suddenly you are required to have regular daily physical exercise. You also find yourself having no time for socialization with friends at popular joints. Your favorite dish is cut off from your daily diet. This is a slow-onset crisis because it builds slowly and eventually attacks you and you have limited capacity to control it.

Another example of a slow-onset crisis is a delay in rains. Assume the rainy season is expected and the rain takes a long time to come. As a community, you will experience a dry season. Then the dry season extends for weeks or months, and eventually, the community experiences a drought where everything dries up due to lack of water or rainfall. As the drought situation intensifies such that people and animals alike lack water, food and pasture, the drought eventually leads to migration, displacement, conflicts, and in extreme cases, death to humans and animals. This becomes a crisis that you cannot control neither are you responsible for its occurrence. However, good leaders and planners are supposed to have the capacity to monitor trends and predict what is likely to occur and take appropriate preparedness actions and mitigation measures.

Another example is an economic crisis. Let us assume that the prices of goods and services have been increasing slowly over a long time. Then the citizens start to protest or riot in the streets of your city. Or, a situation where the price of gasoline keeps rising until all taxis or public transport operators decide to park and stage a countrywide strike that paralyzes all sectors or activities of the country. This is an example of a slow-onset crisis. A divorce is an example of a slow- onset crisis because it does not occur suddenly. When couples marry each other, everything seems okay; relationships between couples, families and friends are exciting and friendly. However, when disagreements, conflicts and differences emerge in a marriage relationship and between couples that started on a good page, a divorce can set in. A divorce is a crisis because it sometimes takes the couple unawares.

A Sudden-onset Crisis

A sudden-onset crisis is one that comes unexpected. Take an example of a terrorist attack in a shopping mall. Or, the shooting of schoolchildren in a United States College? As a parent, what do you do when told your son, daughter or nephew has been killed by the attacker. This is a crisis, which was never expected. Imagine you are travelling on the highway and your car is hit by another speeding vehicle. What do you do?

What about when floodwaters continue to increase and flow downwards from the mountain slopes to a point where water reaches communities, displaces people and even kills them. This unexpected occurrence affects people living in low-lying communities and it is a sudden-onset. What about a fire outbreak in the house and the Fire Service delays to arrive at the burning house to rescue your six-year old twins? The crash of an airplane onto the mountains or sea is a sudden crisis. The derailing of a train that instantly kills passengers is a crisis that suddenly occurs. The collapse of a building due to poor construction and workmanship is a crisis that occurs without expectation. The death of a person through gunshots or heart attack is a sudden-onset crisis.

In November 2013, a cyclone from the Indian Ocean hit parts of Puntland State in Somalia. According to early warning information received before the cyclone hit the region, the report indicated that the speed was over 220 km per hour. When it occurred, it left over 150 people dead. That was a crisis. The cyclone affected several people and messed up their livelihood. Though a cyclone can be predicted, the exact time of occurrence cannot be known. A cyclone and typhoon are also examples of a sudden crisis. The point here is that crisis strikes unexpectedly. Are you ready? Do know what it takes to manage the crisis? Do you know how to recover? Or, even how to overcome it? If you have been wondering what to do, then the ideas, concepts, and principles contained in this book are timely and useful. Use the resources.

Chapter Two

IMPACT OF A CRISIS

*"Managing and navigating through a financial crisis
is no fun at all." ~ **Howard Schultz***

The Impacts of Personal and Global Crises

A personal crisis is one that affects every person on earth. There is no person who has not experienced a crisis. What do you do when your parent dies? What happens when you are taken hostage? A personal crisis can be overcome only if you have a strong foundation. A strong house will stay stable even when a hurricane or cyclone runs over it. However, a house that has a weak foundation is washed away when the torrents hit or strike it. How firm is your foundation? How strong is your foundation? Only strong foundations such as a rock are able to withstand crisis. The key to survival in the midst of a crisis is to have a strong foundation. A personal crisis affects and impacts individuals, families and households by causing the disintegration of systems. It affects people in different ways. For strong persons, the impact of a crisis becomes an opportunity; whereas for weak people, it becomes a curse or a nightmare.

A global crisis is a big one in that it affects organizations, nations or states. No single nation can deal with such a crisis. A global crisis is an event that affects or impacts the whole world, not just one region, continent or nation. It impacts the whole human race and its development, civilization and economic growth. something more catastrophic or cataclysmic can bring about the destruction of the whole world. This can affect or lead to extermination of sections of the world's population. A global crisis is not something horrific that is not isolated to a single organization, nation or location in the entire world or the planet. The global crisis occurs when people have no capacity to buy sufficient goods and services. For businesses, the situation becomes bad where the demand for goods and services reduces; people start to hoard goods, services and money. A global crisis can lead to a recession, or economic or political crisis in which businesses are not performing as expected. Businessmen and women have limited capacity to cope. During a global crisis, people will have a high need for more resources or money and at times governments will be obliged to give out stimulus packages of resources, relief or money to enable people to purchase goods or services so that the economy picks up.

Every Body Suffers from Pain

No one is immune to pain, and it should not be denied when it exists. It is like sickness. However, we can decide to treat the pain. The key is to know we can still lead a productive and meaningful life no matter what the external circumstances are. We need to get positive thoughts. Positive thoughts make you healthier and happier. You need to have a programme for positive thoughts acquisition and maintain it. This way you will often achieve your goals. If you do not get positive thoughts, you will allow negative thoughts to germinate. Negative thinking comes from what we see each day, miserable situations in our world. News or wrong conversations cause negative thoughts to germinate. How do you kill those thoughts? Have affirmations and positive statements.

There is a story of an author called Helen Keller. She was born blind but she was always happy. Once she was asked in an interview: "What is worse than being blind?" She replied, "Having eyes without a vision." I think the best way out in life is always through. Going through the furnace is safer than avoiding it. Facing difficulties head-on is better. Do all you can to emerge from difficulties. Your goal is to stay alive. If you fail, do not say you failed. Say, "I am not a failure if I don't make it. I am successful because I tried." We all experience moments of fear but make a decision to feel the fear and do it anyway. It is not what happens to us but what happens in us. In us are our thoughts, which create our world. Our world comes from ideas. Ideas is everything. Our thoughts produce actions and decisions. Our decisions determine our final destiny. When you have good moods, you feel like you are on top of the world. Positive words make us physically strong. Negative words make us physically weak.

To be strong, you need to believe. Beliefs come from thoughts. Our thoughts in the long run create our character. How stable are you under pressure? Can you smile after a door has been slammed in your face? Can you smile in the face of negative news? How about through disappointments, attacks, or insults? I asked myself one day, "How do you change your life?" Out there, while I was wondering what to do, I made a decision and stood with it. I think at some point in life you must make a decision and stick with it. The other day, I was thinking of some life events. There are things that can completely cause you to go in the right or wrong direction. You can go either up or down. If you keep company with negative thoughts or toxic people, chances are that you will go to the drain or down. How about positive or optimistic people or dreamers? What happens? I have observed that mature people focus on the bright side of the coin of life as the immature do the opposite. What can crying do? What positive impact can it bring? If you have goals, then crying or wailing will cause you to disgrace or delay implementation action. You lose focus, become petty, and start the blame games like the horrible experience of Adam to Eve to Sapient in beautiful Garden of Eden. You must take charge and take responsibility.

There are millions of people out there who have encountered difficult times in their lives but still emerge successful. We are not alone. If we live long enough we shall have testimonies to share. Testimonies are for people who overcame some of the most difficult things in life. Abraham had a testimony after waiting for 25 years for a son. Daniel had a testimony after coming out the den of lions. Shadrach and company came out of the furnace. Jesus came back from the wilderness after the testing of His claim as son of God. Peter was tested at the time of Jesus' arrest and three times, he denied his master. Paul was shipwrecked in the sea and beaten in prison. John was beaten. Stephen's faith was tested with stones on his body. David faced Goliath a giant. Noah was tested to build an ark, which took him 120 years. Can you wait for God for that long? Today's Christians receive a vision or idea from God and they want it happen quickly and easily without going through tests. Testing is not bad or negative. It is a way to know the authenticity of the vision. When being tested do not blame God. Accept tests, challenges and crises as part of life on earth.

The Consequences of Crisis

There are several consequences that a crisis brings to those affected: positive and negative.

The Positive Consequences of a Crisis

The positive impacts include:

- Jobs created.
- Service delivery improved.
- New opportunities emerge.
- New knowledge.
- New insights.
- New behaviors and awareness.
- Innovation and creativity.
- New resources allocated or received.
- New development or humanitarian projects.
- New ideas and plans developed such as emergency and recovery plans.
- New partnerships and relationships emerge.

The Negative Impacts of a Crisis

The negative impacts include:

- Loss of hope.
- Vulnerability.
- Loss of livelihood assets.
- Psychological problems.
- Social problems.
- Economic or financial problems.
- Spiritual problems and doubts.
- Loss of properties.
- Physical stress or depression, fear and anxiety.
- Worry.
- Wailing.
- Weeping.
- Conflict.
- Increased crime rates.
- Domestic violence.
- Marital problems.

How Do You Know That a Crisis Will Happen or Affect You?

A lot of people are always taken unawares when a crisis strikes. To know that a crisis is coming, you or the organization needs to monitor, study and analyze what is happening in the external or internal environment of your system or organization. You will be able to study the early warning signs. There are always pointers, indicators or events that happen to notify you of an imminent crisis. These are called "early warning signs."

46

As we have noted, a crisis can either happen suddenly or occur slowly. Either way, smart leaders and persons must be able to monitor the triggers or signs that could indicate the likelihood of a crisis hitting or affecting families, friends, firms, organizations, communities and businesses or nations. To start the process, early warning signs should be monitored closely. What are early warning signs? These are indicators, pointers or hints or events that signify and indicate that a crisis is likely to occur.

The Signs for Slow-onset Crisis

Take, for example a slow onset crisis like famine. The signs could be:
- Increase in water prices.
- Water shortages for people and livestock's.
- High temperatures above the normal levels.
- Migration of people.
- Displacements.
- Disease outbreaks.
- Increase in food prices.
- Uncontrolled fire outbreaks.
- Increase in fuel prices.
- Increase in criminal activities.
- Riots, conflicts, attacks or domestic violence.
- Unemployment.
- Closure of companies or organizations.

The Signs of Sudden-onset Crises

- Increased rainfall over extended periods of time.
- Water logging.
- Flash floods.
- Mudslides or landslides.

- Changes in prices.
- Disease outbreaks.
- Dysentery, cholera, or acute watery diarrhea.
- Government reports and announcements on potential crisis.

Analyzing Early Warning Signs

A better knowledge and understanding of early warning signs will enable preventive measures to be put in place and could save people from the impacts of the crisis. The role of leaders and leadership is to educate people on the early warning signs and prepare people, organizations, communities, and regions about potential effects of the crisis. Leaders must put systems in place to watch for the signs of a potential crisis. The systems could be collecting and analyzing information used for making informed decisions, choices and preparedness action plans. For organizations, action plans are developed to manage a crisis and reduce its impact. The same applies to families. What about individuals, families or communities?

What do you do when you lose your job to downsizing within an organization? A shift in lifestyle might be required. If you have been having three meals per day, then you might need to reduce this to only two. There might be a need to withdraw from some unproductive activities; such as participating in social functions and engagements. At the time of a crisis, resources usually diminish. For instance, when you lose a job, your source of income and resources has been taken away. Your skills and competencies are not required anymore by the organization that employed you or your partner.

Creativity and Innovation Are Essential in Times of Crisis

A crisis requires a new level of mental adjustments, change in attitudes, behaviors, habits and approaches to situations and life circumstances. A crisis will affect you in such a way that it might require that you assess the resources that you possess. Some resources might have been idle and now a crisis will force you to utilize those resources to survive and thrive. A crisis will require creativity and innovation in solving problems that have been caused. The loss of sources of income requires changes in one's mindset. Assume the livelihood options have been affected; new ways of income generation should be explored through acquiring new set of skills and entrepreneurship acumen.

I have had an opportunity to witness firsthand displaced persons uprooted by conflicts in different parts. In displaced communities, you will notice the emergence of petty traders who were forced out of their communities by sudden crisis with no idea of what they will do next or where they will settle. A crisis forces people to think outside of the box. They become creative and innovative. Dealing with crises requires thinking in creative and innovative ways. The use of innovation and the application of creativity are required during times of crisis. Old thinking void of creativity will not be helpful.

Resource Mobilization During A Crisis

During crisis times, some assets are destroyed; properties get lost and depreciate. The need for resources increases to solve the problems created by a crisis. It is imperative that resource mapping is carried out. Resource mapping is about analyzing which resources are available, accessible and obtainable. It involves asking questions where, how, why, when and which. Let me expound the questions that leaders need to ask.

- Where can we get resources?
- What types of resources are needed?
- When can resources be made available?
- Why do we need resources?
- Who will provide the resources?
- How can the resources be allocated?

What are resources? Resources include properties, houses, cars, computers and land. Other resources could be skills, tools, knowledge, experiences, friends, families, partnership organizations, and people. During the crisis where millions of Jews were taken to concentration camps in Poland towards the middle of the 20th Century; some of the Jews survived because of the skills and knowledge that they possessed. One of the concentration and death camps was known as Sobibor, located in eastern Poland. The authorities would separate families, women and men. Those who had skills and experience in some skills were assigned some work.

However, on 13 October, 1946, a group of prisoners hatched a secret plan to use their skills, training and knowledge to find ways to survive the secret massacre that the world never knew about. The story, *Escape from Sobibor 1987*, is accessible on YouTube. During a crisis, human beings will utilize any available resources to survive. Those who will employ their resources will survive while those who will not put to use their resources will be destroyed.

Those who are resilient will survive, progress and recover from a crisis.

When I was in high school, there was a common saying that we used with a group of friends. It goes like this, "When the going gets tough, only the tough get going." In other words, when crisis hits only those with resilience will survive and recover. Among the Japanese and Chinese, the use of the word crisis is not pronounced or talked about. Instead, when a crisis hits, they talk of opportunity.

The Practical Actions to Take During a Crisis

1. Leaders and followers must hold discussions on plans, strategies and actions.
2. Leaders must organize brainstorming discussions with the teams or leaders regarding how to solve the crisis.
3. Leaders must identify team leaders, teammates, group members or individuals with talents, skills and knowledge in certain fields.
4. Leaders must assign tasks and responsibilities to accomplish certain goals.
5. Leaders must make sure that deadlines for activity implementation are set and determined.
6. Leaders must identify various activities that will improve or save the situation.
7. Leaders and individuals need to take on calculated risks and minimize danger.
8. Leaders must employ and use the already available resources, tools, equipment, people and skills.

9. Leaders must learn to make tough decisions that can save the situations and save lives that are in danger due to crisis.
10. Leaders and followers must share information and keep all stakeholders informed on next steps, actions or decisions.
11. Leaders must carry our activities rapidly, quickly, appropriately and responsibly.

A Crisis as an Opportunity

A lot of people think that crisis has only a negative side. A crisis has both a negative and positive side. A crisis comes with negative and positive effects. When terrorists attacked the World Trade Center on 11 September 2001, there was chaos and confusion in New York City. The terrorists took the advantage of relaxed security measures to gain entry into the airplanes with their explosives and directed the pilots to fly in the direction of the skyscrapers of the Twin Towers of World Trade Center. Within hours, one of the unexpected crises that would forever change the world politics had just happened like a movie in the United States.

As the world came to terms with the crisis and its after effects, some of creative, innovative and design thinkers swung into action. They used the crisis as an opportunity to design and invent screening machines and other security gadgets at the airports. As other people were still looking at a crisis as a negative event, others used it as an opportunity to make millions of dollars, created companies, jobs, new investments and more businesses.

To me a crisis could mean any of the following:

- *Crisis is not only a negative event, but an opportunity as well.*
- *Crisis is the source of creativity.*
- *Crisis is the source of new ideas and the mother of innovation.*

True leaders never panic during times of crisis, but instead they use it as an opportunity for planning a new response. They use it as one of the best opportunities that gets presented to them to find new ways to solve problems created by the crisis. Individuals and leaders alike must learn to maximize the benefits of crisis for progress, creation of new businesses and expand their horizons. If your employer decides to lay 40 percent of its labor force, those laid off or released from their jobs could use the crisis to create better jobs or businesses. It is the duty of leaders to work with followers to explore opportunities.

In all crises that happens, there will be an opportunity. Crisis forces people to think in different ways to solve problems that inflict pain and cause misery. Leaders use the opportunity to plan new projects, ventures or set a new direction for the organization. Leaders plan when a crisis hits. Leaders develop a new vision.

What You Call a Thing is What It Becomes

I have come to believe that a thing become whatever it is labelled as. If you call a crisis a crisis, it will be a crisis. If you turn around to call it an opportunity, it will be viewed as an opportunity. Proverbs 23:7 says, *"For as he thinks in his heart, so is he ..."* We have already explored the positive and negative impacts and effects of a crisis. What should leaders teach followers in times of crisis? I believe in times of crisis leaders must preach confidence and faith to people affected or impacted by the crisis. Paul, the leader of the early community of believers in Philippi said the following words:

Do not be anxious about anything, but in every situation, by prayer and petition, with thanksgiving, present your requests to God. And the peace of God, which transcends all understanding, will guard your hearts and your minds in Christ Jesus. (Philippians 4:6-7)

The historical account gives insights that the early believers in Philippi were often coming under attacks and crisis from authorities or governments of the day. We have already seen that during crisis, people become anxious about anything e.g., the news, death of a loved one, etc.

A Crisis Will Affect Everyone at Some Point in Life; Nobody is Immune

There are some folks who believe that crisis is meant for others and not them. They believe that bad things happen to bad people while good things happen to good people. This is false knowledge and understanding. A crisis will affect every one either directly or indirectly. Crisis respects nobody. When United States government reported in 2008 that there was a financial crisis facing its nation, some people never thought it would affect China, Europe or Africa. Do you know what happened? It affected the entire world; it was known as a global financial crisis. How did this happen?

When the businesses and companies collapsed in America in 2008, workers were laid off and taxpayers were unable to pay their taxes, which also affected the economy. The crisis affected every corner of the planet. Workers in India, China and Africa lost their jobs because of events in America. The great nations such as G8, or G20 had to hold meetings in Brussels, Belgium to find ways to mitigate the effect of global financial crisis. The Arab states, China, Australia and Africa were equally affected by global financial crisis. You might be thinking that a financial crisis or terrorism impacts only nations. The fact is that organizations both humanitarian and developmental ones were also impacted by the global financial crisis because of donors failing to make their financial contributions or donations. The defense and security budgets in most countries have doubled and affecting the budgets of other sectors because of the global terror threats. Crisis does not segregate or discriminate, it affects everybody. Crisis as we have seen affects every person; but only those people with strong foundations and excellent at planning will emerge out of crisis.

The Wise and Foolish Builders

Jesus said the following words to His disciples:

Therefore, everyone who hears these words of mine and puts them into practice is like a wise man who built his house on the rock. But everyone who hears these words of mine and does not put them into practice is like a foolish man who built his house on sand. The rain came down, the streams rose, and the winds blew and beat against that house, and it fell with a great crash. When Jesus had finished saying these things, the crowds were amazed at his teaching, because he taught as one who had authority, and not as their teachers of the law. (Mathew 7: 24-29)

I have travelled to many countries in the world and I have come to a simple and practical conclusion: There are millions of men and women walking on planet who qualify as either wise or foolish builders. The most dangerous thing in life is the lack of wisdom. The worst thing in life is foolishness. The two probably are the cause of many problems in the world. Wise people make right decisions as the foolish ones make wrong decisions. Decisions create our world.

The leader of twelve apostles told the followers that if you hear the words and ideas that He presented to them, they must practice those ideas. Jesus equated those who practice those ideas to the wise man who built his house on the rock. What happens when you build the house on the rock? A rock is often very difficult to dismantle. It requires heavy equipment to pull the rock down. Are you wise? Do you have wisdom? If you lack it, you need to go get wisdom. Go back to school and pursue more education to gain knowledge, understand it and apply it as wisdom. When you apply wisdom, you will be a wise person. In the above discourse, Jesus turned the story upside down. The foolish builders built their houses on the sand that was easily washed away by the rains, floods or winds. I have said earlier that a storm does not respect people, institutions, groups or nations. Storms affect everyone.

Crisis Leads to Promotion and Leadership

David took the Philistine's head and brought it to Jerusalem; he put the Philistine's weapons in his own tent. As Saul watched David going out to meet the Philistine, he said to Abner, commander of the army, "Abner, whose son is that young man?" Abner replied, "As surely as you live, Your Majesty, I don't know." The king said, "Find out whose son this young man is." As soon as David returned from killing the Philistine, Abner took him and brought him before Saul, with David still holding the Philistine's head. "Whose son are you, young man?" Saul asked him. David said, "I am the son of your servant Jesse of Bethlehem. (I Samuel 17:54-58)

There was a crisis between the Israelites and Philistines as recorded in the above text. David defeated Goliath and carried the head to the palace. This crisis was the turning point of the politics of the day in Israel where Saul was the king. Crisis produces many good things, including promotions.

Courage in Times of Trials or Crisis

There many examples of individuals who were able to stand up in the midst of crisis. Paul is an example as show below:

After they had gone a long time without food, Paul stood up before them and said: "Men, you should have taken my advice not to sail from Crete; then you would have spared yourselves this damage and loss. But now I urge you to keep up your courage, because not one of you will be lost; only the ship will be destroyed. Last nights an angel of the God to whom I belong and whom I serve stood beside me and said, 'Do not be afraid, Paul. You must stand trial before Caesar; and God has graciously given you the lives of all who sail with you.' So keep up your courage, men, for I have faith in God that it will happen just as he told me. Nevertheless, we must run aground on some island. (Acts 27:21-26)

What is the Source of Paul's Confidence?

- Paul had faith in God.
- Paul had information, which other people did not know about.
- Paul had conviction and courage.

Chapter Three

HOW DO LEADERS OVERCOME CRISIS?

*"In a time of domestic crisis, men of goodwill and generosity should be able to unite regardless of party or politics." ~ **John F. Kennedy***

The 2008 Global Financial Crisis

In the year 2008 when former US President, Barack Obama, was voted into office, the whole world was going through a deep global financial crisis. I recall watching Barack Obama's victory speech in a tiny hotel in the Kabale town (often referred as the "Switzerland of Uganda" because of the similarities with Switzerland in terms of climate and weather). At that time, Obama's slogan was: "Yes, we can." I do not know if everyone walking on the planet understood what that meant. This somewhat deep financial crisis appears more frequently than people imagine. From what I have observed since the year 2008, financial crises have continued to affect nations, governments, companies more frequently than people or leaders expect. Crisis does affect everyone.

Once more, it affects companies and nations that are going through rapid change or transformation as a result of increased competition and experience changes in politics, economics, social, technological and environmental and other aspects of life. Crisis is a product of change. Whenever there is a change, there will likely be a crisis. When things are normal, there is no crisis. When things become abnormal, there will be change that can create a crisis.

The point here is that, people in every nation or company do not like crises of any sort. The dictionary meaning of crisis is: "an upheaval or turning point that causes a decisive change that can be either worse or better." However, the word "crisis" is always seen with a negative lens or has a negative meaning attached to it. The moment the word "crisis" is mentioned, straight away the people or leaders assume that a disaster is coming or has occurred already. Most of the people dread or fear crisis. That happens to all, including leaders of countries, business organizations or families. The reasons for fear of crisis are diverse, such as the impact it brings and how equipped people are to guard against it. Leaders have a natural leadership obligation to protect or guard their countries or companies from crisis of any nature.

Destabilization of Comfort Zone by Rapid Change

Throughout human history of existence, human are creatures of tradition and like to live in a place known as "comfort zone." The comfort zone is a place of the familiar where nothing changes. But the reality or truth about living on earth is that change will happen unexpectedly it can be rapid or slow. Rapid change in politics, economy, technology, society or environment will cause a crisis. The nations or organizations that are able to withstand rapid crises are stronger while those that collapse or fail to standup are weaker. This means that if your organization is strong, it will deal with change or crisis but the opposite is also true.

To put it differently, organizations are like organisms. They exist in the environment. If the organism is strong or lacks strength, change can affect it. A strong organism will withstand crisis while a weak organism can be destroyed by it. The weaker the organization, the easier it will be destroyed or killed. The phenomenon that is described above does apply to both people and the organization alike. People or organizations that prepare to deal with crisis are always motivated by crisis as a good occurrence. Those people or organizations that dread it will collapse, fall ill, and disappear. For organizations, they can end up becoming bankrupt and close operations.

When I talk about a strong organization or organism, it does not mean strength of body or muscles. It simply means the strength to respond to change and the capacity to handle the rapid change creates a crisis. There are three questions that are related that I want you to think about: How do human get diseases: How do organisms get diseases; How do organizational diseases occur? In other words, how do problems occur? Let me give you an example: If you are exposed to cold or heavy winds, you know what will happen to you, don't you? You will catch a cold, flu or fever. Why? There is change in the environment to which you are exposed. I mentioned earlier that a crisis is a result of a change in the conditions. The problems or diseases that affect people or organizations are a direct result of change. If you want to be able to handle crisis, you must understand the concept of change. The cause of problems must be studied by the changes that have occurred in the past.

What must be noted here is that change is not something that is new. Change is nothing new. Change has existed for several centuries. The only new occurrence is the pace or the rate of change, where it is accelerating faster than it was years before. Imagine the advent of communication systems. Inventions have created many types of phones and today, we have the iPhone. In a few years to come, there will be new models.

In order to manage change, especially rapid change, strategic choices, actions and decisions must be made. Every generation has experienced a share of its change. The people that lived before us might have made changes in their lives, such as moving from one place to another, changing careers to better their lives, etc. These I call strategic decisions. That means every season they faced or change they encountered led made them to make strategic decisions. For instance, if there were a lack of pasture or water for the nomads, they would travel long distances in search of it. This is what I call change. It is not new; it has happened before. If there was war or disease outbreak, strategic decisions were made.

The Nature of Change and Its Effects

The rate of increase of change comes with its own effects. Whenever change occurs, certainly, problems will emerge. What do you do when the new situations occur? How do you face new conditions? When the change accelerates, the problems also increase in the manner they attack us or organizations. Is there a human being who has no problems? The only person without a problem is a human resting in the cemetery! Every person who is alive has a problem or problems. That means every person has problems they can or cannot handle. If they fail to handle problems, they fall behind faster than they are able to handle the problems and that is what causes people to be stressed.

However, when solutions to problems are identified, the same solution becomes another source of problems. Let me give you an example. Assume you had a problem going to work or the office and you decided to buy a vehicle. That vehicle is a solution to the transport problem on one side, but on the other side, it is a problem. It will require maintenance, servicing or fuel on daily basis. When an organization is able to solve its problems, then what happens next? The solution causes change and that change causes new problems. Now, the more we solve problems, the more problems emerge. The result is that as problems are solved new problems emerge because there is some new change.

The truth is this: People never want problems. Why don't people or organizations want problems? They do not want change. Change comes with its own problems or challenges. Many political, religious, system, leaders or organizations have ideologies that they will solve people's problems but that is not necessarily true. As they solve problems, new problems will emerge. If people or organizations do not expect change, then that means they are not living organism. Living organisms are exposed to environments all of the time, which is always experiencing changes. Problems stop when there is no change. The truth about problems is they are only stopped when no new change occurs and that happens when people or organizations die. Think about that for a minute. The only person who has no problems resides in the cemetery and there is nothing that happens in the cemetery. Being alive simply means having problems. That also means life is full of problems. If you are not having any problems right now, do not worry; the problems are taking their time but they will visit you. Get ready because problems are on the way. When there is no life, it means there are no changes and also no problems. Problems are a result of living and a result of change. If the rate of change is faster in your family or organization, then you will encounter multiple problems.

What Should You Expect as an Individual or a Company?

You should expect problems. Why? You are a living organism. Expecting problems must be a normal thing that happens to an individual or organization. If your company is growing at a higher rate or proportion, then you must be experiencing change and the change will come with problems. It is normal to have problems and that should not come as a surprise. When you are able to change normally, you are having normal problems.

The test comes when you as organization or leader fail to handle the problems that have been caused by change. When you are unable to handle problems normally then your problems have become abnormal problems. When also you continue being complacent in handling the abnormal problems, they end up becoming fatal problems. Fatal problems are produced by abnormal problems. It must be noted that problems change in the level of their severity as time passes by. When problems are not solved immediately, they become abnormal and later move to the fatal phase. Take an example of a person who has a normal weight. Normal weight is okay. But when it becomes abnormal, then abnormal problems are coming and if not handled, they become fatal.

Remember this statement: As you become bigger, your capacity to handle problems should also increase and get bigger. Therefore, you are as big as the problems you have the capacity to handle. When you have problems, it does not mean you will die, it means there is change. Change leads to growth, pain, and loss. To put as mathematic equation, it becomes;

Change	=	Growth
Growth	=	Pain
Pain	=	Loss
Change	=	Loss
Change	=	Crisis
Crisis	=	Growth

Let us assume that this year you are starting your investment such as a school, hospital or company. You might start well and face some problems that you solve. As the number of clients increases, you will experience bigger problems that you will also manage to handle. Why do problems get bigger? Because you are growing and changes are happening. Whenever you have few problems, it means your strength is weakening and declining. Age is catching up with you. The reverse is also true: If you have bigger problems and you are able to handle them, it means you are growing; your strength is becoming stronger and increasing. When you fail to handle big problems, you are dying slowly but surely.

Whenever there is change, do you have the capacity to deal with it? The way you deal with change depends on the organism-you! If the leader has capacity to handle problems, then it means they are not more problems but opportunities. The truth and reality of living is that where there is a problem, there is an opportunity. Among the Chinese people, problem and opportunity are the same. There is no difference among those words. That does not make any sense among different people of the world. What opportunities are you seeing from the problems you are experiencing? If someone is having a problem, then there is an opportunity in there. If you can address the problem, then you have the opportunity. Your problem is an opportunity in the waiting.

Remember that every change comes with problems that are also opportunities. It all depends on how you see or view the situation. Your response to it makes it a problem or an opportunity. How does this come about? A problem emerges as a problem if nothing is done, but if you decide to react carefully, it will become an opportunity. What do you think?

Chapter Four

THE POWER OF INTEGRATION, LEADERSHIP AND MANAGEMENT OF CRISES

"When times are tough and people are frustrated and angry and hurting and uncertain, the politics of constant conflict may be good, but what is good politics does not necessarily work in the real world. What works in the real world is cooperation." **- President William J. Clinton**

The Disintegration Process of Systems And Organizations

This is a word that is normally not talked about. Nobody likes to talk about disintegration. When problems start attacking your family or organization, it implies that there is something that is disintegrating. When your automobile is not functioning effectively as expected, then something is falling apart. If your physician tells you that you have cancer or tumor it also means that something is disintegrating. It also means that there are some parts of the body that are falling apart. If you are experiencing emotional problems, it means there is some disintegration. If the business is not doing well, it simply means that something is wrong or some things are falling apart. These implies that problems are a result of disintegration.

When families experience problems, things start to fall apart, right? What about organizations? What about nations? When civil war broke out in Somalia in the 1990s, things fell apart, not so? What happened when war erupted in Syria, Iraq, South Sudan or Afghanistan? Things have fallen apart or disintegrated. When crises hit the Arab nations of Libya, Tunisia and Egypt in the early years after 2011, things fell apart. There was disintegration, right? We also talk of countries that have fallen apart. We have families that have disintegrated. When companies are unable to deal with change, things will fall apart. There will be disintegration.

Can you imagine the scenario when the rate of change is fastest? What happens? Things will start falling apart. If the problems are more than expected, then disintegration will be the expected result. The faster the changes, the more problems will be experienced. The higher rate of change in a family, organization or even a nation will cause more problems. In times of crisis, the desire to solve problems with urgency and rapidly becomes paramount. Why? The need to rescue the situation. It also requires quick action and timely reaction. The challenge is that not all humans are designed that way.

What Do You Do When There Is Disintegration?

I believe leaders are born and tested when things are falling apart. True leaders emerge during this period. They emerge to take up responsibility, results but also carry the blame. In such situations, decisions must be made on what must be done. What are you going to do when you have been told things are falling apart? Remember, people are different with different leadership styles, management styles, personalities, interests, motives and thoughts. They also have different needs that have to be handled separately. The challenge is that pressure sets in; stress might manifest, which also increases more pain, suffering and further disintegration. When the external forces to the organization or countries come and cause rapid disintegration, organizations or countries will also fall apart. The rapid changes in families, businesses, or organizations alike will cause disintegration.

What Caused the Global Financial Crisis of 2008 in the USA?

To answer this question would require scholarly research. I want to explain it so that anyone can also understand. After all, millions of people do not like to research. Research is seen as a burden. Let us refresh our memory. USA is the richest nation in the world. It is a super power. What really happened? Senator Barack Obama said,

This financial crisis is a direct result of the greed and irresponsibility that has dominated Washington and Wall Street for years. It's the result of speculators who gamed the system, regulators who looked the other way, and lobbyists who bought their way into our government (Nevado, R. September 30, 2008).

According to reports, the decade before 2008 financial crisis, many Americans took mortgages well beyond their capacity and means. They also assumed that the value of mortgages or homes bought using bank funds would continue to appreciate in financial terms, without thinking that the situations would change. Risk analysis was not done effectively. Several financial institutions gave out loans without property analysis, scrutiny and foresight of what would be the future like. The insurance companies and stock buyers also were not analytical enough to assess the implications. Everything was going good and nothing was bad.

But what happened? Things started falling apart in the banking, insurance or stock market sectors within the USA economy. This is what I call disintegration. It affected the borrowers, investors, bankers, and insurance companies. Nobody was able to nip it in the bud. Before long, the systems collapsed and things fell apart and affected different parts of the world. The cause of global financial crisis was slowly caused by disintegration that started without anyone taking a keen step to stop it. The crisis was also due to falling in the value of the mortgages that investors expected to keep rising.

However, what usually happens in circumstances such as those is that lies will be told and statistics can be used to back up the lies. Whenever there is something wrong, statistics are used to show the size or magnitude of the situation. Take the case of Syria; numbers (statistics) show the affected people by crisis. Take the case of Somalia; statistics show that things are bad. Everywhere you go; numbers will be used to tell lies. One thing that is so true about statistics is that authorities can play with the figures. Figures can be adjusted upwards or downwards. In other words, figures can be altered or manipulated. As a result of one event leading to another, a chain reaction or cumulative effect will be produced. The cumulative effect is what I consider a domino effect. A domino effect is produced when there are interlinked sequences of events produced from small events occurring in successive manner. For instance, displacements create congestion of people in an area or outbreak of diseases.

Furthermore, I believe some crises are also caused by reckless behavior and greedy practices. Greed is good and bad. The good side of greed is that it serves as a motivator for individuals to work and fuel the economies forward. The downside of greed is that it can lead to mismanagement and disintegration where leaders take opportunities for personal gain or enrichment.

Key Takeaways
- *Every problem is caused when there is disintegration resulting from change.*
- *A crisis manifests whenever prolonged and untreated causes of disintegration have not been addressed or managed.*

Going back to the global financial crisis, I would like to refresh your memory. The global financial crisis was caused by changes in systems, structures and policies. The changes produced disintegration because of failure to handle the situation appropriately. Why? There was no history of a precedent to be used to do things in a different manner. This means what was initially a normal problem turned to become abnormal problem and produced a crisis. A crisis is produced when normal problems become abnormal problems.

The country of Somalia fell apart in 1991. Iraq went to war in 2003 and the same is true of Afghanistan. Syrian uprising started in 2011 during what was referred to as the Arab spring. South Sudan returned to war when two leaders, Salva Kiir and Riek Machar, fell apart. The government of national unity disintegrated.

When things fall apart, what should be the solution? What do you do when things are falling apart? When a family is falling apart? When friendships are disintegrating? It means change is happening. Change always causes problems. You will also find people calling for the formation of the government of national unity. What do they mean by that? Do you know what that means? In essence, they are calling for integration.

The way to avoid crises proactively is to pay attention to how integration is managed. An organization that is fully integrated has capacity to withstand any external change or threat than those who are not already disintegrating. An integrated family can stand against any changes compared to a disintegrated one. Proactive approach is needed to avoid disintegration. If your car is having mechanical problems and it makes noise when it is being driven, what do you do? Simple! Go to the mechanic or garage so that mechanics examine the situation and stop disintegration. How? By putting things together and making it whole again.

But for most of us, when change comes, our way of handling is to react to it. This is not a good way. Reacting to change is dangerous. It means you never observed the signs and symptoms of change happening. There will always be "noise or problems unidentified" before disintegration. If you are sober and careful enough, you can prepare ahead. This is what I call preparedness. If nothing is done when signs are blinking like the vehicle indicators, a crisis will happen. Why? No action was taken in the first place. For an organization, if the crisis is not handled carefully, ensuring integration, it can lead to the demise of the organization. For communities, if crisis where there are indicators of drought, the demise of people will be unavoidable. Integration can be attained by being proactive or reactive. You choose which one. Life is a choice. You or your organization must decide.

How you deal with it matters. You either proactive or reactive. The only problem I notice is the differences in the speed of taking actions and the degree of complexity. If you fail to deal with disintegration early enough, it will take long to fix it. It also becomes more complex. The longer you take in achieving integration, more sub systems emerge and problems that are more complex will emerge, and solving these becomes even more complex.

I remember working in Somalia from 2012 to 2015. When I arrived in Somalia, I read the history of that beautiful country with its precious people, the Somalis. I discovered that things fell apart in 1991 when the first government collapsed. What followed was more disintegration. Now the so-called "states" were created. Somaliland region became a state of its own. Puntland became another state of its own, and many regions became states of their own. Each had its own army, police, parliament and "presidents." What happened? Problems became complex, and up until today, the country is unable to deal with complex subsystem problems. Achieving successful integration when subsystems have disintegrated is an uphill undertaking or endeavor.

Key Takeaways
- *Integration is the treatment for disintegration done in a proactive manner.*
- *Learn to be proactive and avoid reactive approach to problems.*
- *Monitoring signs will help prediction of problems and get solutions before a crisis happens.*

What do I mean by treatment? Take the analogy of the car with mechanic. If the car has problems, the treatment is looking for what is falling off or broken and fixing it. This is why mechanics fix spare parts to vehicles when things are falling apart. When things are not working properly, the solution is to find out the best efficient and effective way to make work together again. What does this require? To me it requires management. The heading of this chapter has something related to dominion and management command! I will come back to that in a short while.

To avoid having problems become abnormal and manifesting into a crisis, you have to learn the basics of management. A strong organization is one that has strong management. A weak one has weakness in management. How do you have strong management? To me this is being proactive in solving problems. Being proactive is always the best way to handle problems. Do not wait for things to fall apart and then act or react. You need to do contingency response planning. When you are proactive, nothing will surprise you. Being proactive makes you ready to deal with a problem. The good thing about being proactive is that your energy and time will be used in a good way. A crisis is usually a problem that you have ignored before it hits you. Problems usually hit you in the stomach but a crisis will bring you down to your knees. Do you see the difference? Never wait until things start falling apart. Be proactive.

Key Takeaway

- *Surviving a crisis requires that you or the organization never wait until things start disintegrating. Instead, be proactive.*

An Analogy

A parent started to notice that their son was not interested in education but instead wanted to watch movies daily. They ignored it. They said that he likes to watch movies. Did they check the movies the son was watching? No! Like most of us, we never check. Unfortunately, the police arrested the boy as part of criminal gang that had been terrorizing the community. The point is never wait until crisis happens. The same is also true with your organization. You should not wait for the problems to appear in the "door." It is always better to prepare early in advance. Most problems are avoidable. So that when problems come to you, you say, "I have been waiting for you and I am ready to take you on."

Doing Nothing: What to Do When Faced with Unprecedented Levels of Crisis

Some people make the worst of all choices. When signs of disintegration start showing up, they never bother. They sit and wait. This is a bad approach. Sometimes they freeze in their fear. Some people accuse what is happening around them. They blame the environment. They blame their past or background. They cover up things as if nothing is happening. At times, they blame the wind, storms or the weather. This is dangerous. For organizations; it can cause demise, and for humans it can cause "morbidity or mortality."

What must be noted is that change always causes problems depending on how you look at the change. If you are proactive, change will not affect you that much, but the reverse is also true. The source of problems in real sense is increasing rate of change or disintegration. When no action is taken and no treatment is provided, eventually problems will end up causing a crisis. Some people literally do nothing when change is happening. They think or imagine it will just pass, that the storm will clear off.

What about a personal crisis? What do you do? Whenever there is a personal crisis, you experience pain. If you go to the doctor, they will prescribe some actions to be taken. They examine you. They investigate. They take blood samples. They carry out tests. The results are studied. Conclusions are made. Years back, I was not feeling well. I used to have back pain. I used to blame my office chair. The pain continued until I went to the doctors. They examined me. They did what I have written up in this paragraph. They found out that some things were falling apart. They told me, if I you do not take the following actions that I will disintegrate. Can you imagine disintegrating? Therefore, I had to take an action. But, doing nothing was one choice I could have made.

Another Analogy

Suppose you are driving and you reach a T-junction or intersection of a major high way or road. What must you do? What you have just encountered is a change. Somethings totally different has happened. Something new. It requires you to take a decision. You have choices: Turning left or right, going backward, or forward. You decide. If you decide not to decide (e.g. by saying you do not know what to do or say or lack the energy or information), you will still have made a decision. Your choices and decisions determine where you will end up in life.

Key Takeaways

- *Your choices and decisions determine where you will end up.*
- *Arriving to a given destination depends on choices or decisions made.*

However, the worst thing to do is not to decide. You will be cautious as you make the decisions. There is statement I heard years back from an American trainer who was part of the United Nations security, when I worked in Northern Uganda at the height of the Joseph Kony war. If you do not know about this war, please just Google it. The training was a security training for working in High Risky Environment.

During the training, the American trainer used an American expression: "Even if you are on the right road, if you just stand there, you may be run over by a truck." Whenever there is a crisis or a problem, you should do something. The worst thing is doing nothing. What happens? You experience an increase in pain. That pain may lead to fear! If you decide not to decide, you have made a decision and a choice. Doing nothing is also making a decision.

Key Takeaways
- *Doing nothing in any situation is also a decision.*
- *If you decide to do nothing, you have also made a decision.*
- *The Implications of Doing Nothing, No Decision or Action*

The normal reaction that occurs to most people during a crisis is to do nothing. Whenever you decide to do nothing, you will end up as a victim. A victim is an individual who watches things happen and they are bewildered. What might these folks say? What might they think? Things happen to them. They are powerless in their speech and actions. They are reactive. During a crisis, you do not want to be reactive. Instead, you want to be one who takes action. You want to be proactive. Do not just talk about doing something; do it! Be a planner. That is the best response to a crisis.

A Story of Mary Kay, an American Entrepreneur

This lady began from scratch but ended up establishing a large cosmetics empire that deals in cosmetics and personal care products (Wikipedia). She started from nothing but built a company worthy millions of dollars. They asked her about the secret to her success, and here is her reply: "Do you want to see the scars on my knees? It is the secret to my success!" What a reply or an answer that was given! Success is not about how many times you fall down. Instead, success is how much faster and quicker you stand up after a fall."

Remember this very important message. Everybody falls and everybody fails. Everybody will sooner or later fall or fail. It will be sooner or later before another person falls. But some people fall frequently, but to become successful, we must learn to dare and take risks. When there is disintegration or when a crisis has occurred you will soon come to a realization that you are falling and your success is being challenged or tested. It is the time to run faster than other people or competitors to avoid a lion from devouring you. Have you watched lions chasing the prey in the jungle? You will notice that the weaker ones without the ability to run faster will be captured, killed, destroyed and eaten. The same is true with you or your organization.

On the other hand, if you are weak, you know the consequences or outcomes. If you are slow, you can predict the future. In crisis times, you need to be faster or else you will become a "victim." You will be overpowered. When lions attack other wild animals, a crisis suddenly erupts. During a crisis, you should not freeze; when you fall, you should try to get up or run faster. What else can you do? It is the time for moving faster so that when the lion is chasing you, you survive and some other "person" is eaten.

The Westgate Mall Attack by Al Shabaab Terrorists in Kenya

The suspected Al Shabaab terrorists battling with Somalia government carried out a deadly attack at the Westgate Mall in Nairobi on 23 September 2013. The attack left over 67 people dead and hundreds injured. Property worth over $200,000 was destroyed. Can you imagine the cost of a crisis? How would you feel if you are one of the many who lost millions of dollars? You need to study these experiences by going to the University of Life. The University of Life or School of Life can explain to you much more of what you must do. What if you lost $150,000? How do you respond? Please note that only a few people can afford to pay education worthy of that amount. I believe I am one of the few. Looking from that angle, let me drive the point home. If you pay tuition for a course or program, your goal must be passing the course. Not so? Have you passed the course? What happened? What did you learn from the course taught by the University of Life? Or are you among those who failed the course?

A crisis must be interpreted from the point of view as a course studied and taken from the University of Life. Every problem must be viewed as a course. There is tuition paid to study the course. When you go to a university, you study a course or program. Either you have a scholarship or you will sponsor yourself. My question is what did you learn from the crisis or problem? What value or benefit accrued from the course that you took? The most important thing is to determine the knowledge acquired, the skills and competencies harvested and carried home from the University of Life. Was there tuition or fees wasted when you studied at the University of Life? What did you learn from the University of Life? The most important issue to walk away with is learning from the experiences of life and apply those lessons to life's problems.

Key Takeaways
- *Use a crisis as a learning opportunity to advance forward or move up but never down.*
- *Use every crisis as the greatest opportunity for learning and gaining valuable lessons to apply in life.*

It is important to be proactive as crisis looms. Develop the capacity to act with urgency. You should be moving forward and avoid stopping to move. How do you ensure integration during the moments of crisis or rapid change? As a leader or manager, you will need to fight against disintegration that is caused by change. True leaders develop capacity to ensure integration and avoid disintegration.

If an organization is faced with a crisis that must be produced by change. Leaders and managers in the organizations must fight to make sure the organization is integrated during the moments of rapid change. Change always brings disintegration.

Therefore, what should be done as a leader or manager during the times of crises? That is the time when a leader must emerge and model integrity and creativity. A leader needs to keep the organization together and integrated. My question is this: Can you stay together as a single entity? If an effective leader leads an organization, the organization will keep integrated and stay together. That is when all resources must be used to fight the common enemy of crises. Fighting together requires having organizational members who are trustworthy.

However, for organizations that are not effectively managed or those that I referred earlier as "weak organism" in which members have no trust for one another, there will be fear of the enemy. When the crisis is attacking the organization, it is easy for the enemy to destroy the organizations. What happens when the enemy attacks? It can kill everybody in the organization. Therefore, in times or moments of crisis as any other times, there must be trust.

How Does Integration Work And Keep the Organization Strong?

I recall in the year 1986/7 my father lost all his wealth including assets like a tractor and cattle during the war. Our relatives and neighbors also lost their wealth, which included cattle. In my culture in Uganda, someone with cattle is considered as a wealthy person. I recall we reached a point when we sometimes did not have food and life was hard. My father was never discouraged by what was going on. He was fine all the time. As I grew up, I asked him," What made you strong during those times when you lost everything?" I recall his answer; he said, "I did not lose all things. I lost cattle and a tractor only, but still have my faith and life." He said, " When faith is lost, life is also lost."

Can you have that attitude when you lose your money or job? One of the things I saw from my father is that he never lost his real assets. The assets that he was referring to included his personal health, family and friendships. He used to go to meet his brothers and relatives, which kept him strong. One thing I recall was that when he kept his real assets, he was able to recover what he lost. After the war, my father was again able to gain what he lost. It is important to note the following; when there is a crisis, the people will lose not only money but also other things such as their health; families that disintegrate will also lose their close friends.

In any crisis, priority must be to take care of your health, family and friendships. The pressure of crisis can cause you to experience pain, stress and make you vulnerable to sickness. The most important thing is to keep integrated. Let me say it in another way:

"Keep together." I want to give you a practical example. Have you ever considered instructions given when you enter an airplane? You will be told that if there is an emergency with lack of oxygen, you will be told to use the oxygen mask that will fall automatically from a panel above your seat. Even when you are travelling with infants, they will tell you to help yourself first. I used to wonder why they say something like that. I finally figured out the answer. You are told to put on your mask first before helping others. Why? The answer is that when you are falling apart or when there is a crisis, you will need to take care of yourself first so you can help others later.

What Else Do You Need to do During Crisis?

1. Sometimes you might need to slow down and engage in "slow thinking," which helps you to meditate.
2. Never panic.
3. Use deep breathing or other relaxation methods to stay calm.
4. Stay together as a family or organization.
5. Provide hope to those who are hopeless.
6. Apply leadership.
7. Call and contact your friends. Ask for their perspectives and support.
8. Focus on also of integrating the organization.
9. Work to bring hope and reduce fear.
10. Always be honest.
11. Be accountable and truthful.
12. Never deny the fact that there is a crisis. Instead, find ways to deal with it.
13. Never make false promises.

Chapter Five

FIFTEEN PRACTICAL WAYS FOR OVERCOMING CRISES

"What does not kill you makes you stronger."

~ Anonymous

The Practical Ways to Overcome Any Crisis

The section below, gives you various ways in which you can use to deal with and overcome any crisis. There are many ways to overcome a crisis. But what does it mean to overcome? Overcome means to defeat. It means to succeed in controlling something. Crises can be overcome but all this required knowledge of certain ways and approaches. In this chapter, I will expound on the best strategies that you can use. The aim is for you as a leader or an organization to emerge out of crisis without it destroying you. The ways include:

1. Integration

One of the approaches to crisis management is what I have been writing about, integration. I believe you need to apply this concept to a crisis. Through integration in all dimensions of both personal and professional life, including your family, friends, organizational employees and clients, you will be able to survive the onslaught of a crisis. How? You will become stronger than before the crisis hit you. The more integration happens, the stronger you will become after you emerge from the crisis. That is why you will see that families that are united will always overcome any crisis or adversity as compared to those that are divided. Have you noticed that in your life?

As a matter of fact, a crisis might even turn out as the best thing that ever happened to you and your organization. Why? You might notice the following as major outcomes of a crisis or adversity:

- Strengthened your family ties' made you or your family or organization stronger than before the crisis.
- Increased stability, determination, focus, and resolution.
- Heightened discipline and humility.
- Enhanced and reinforced relationships with clients, employees or stakeholders because you are fighting a common enemy, "a disaster."
- Boosted your wisdom by lessons learned from the "University of Life." You are now a wise person.
- Increased your motivation to take action.
- Revealed your true abilities and colors of true leaders.

However, some people always react to a crisis by attributing all the causes of crises or problems to outside of what they can control. This is a bad way of reacting to problems. This attitude will cause you to be destroyed or cause your organization to close down. Most people always take the easy way of avoiding a crisis. You must be able to deal with problems and take control. During times of crisis, some people blame others, outside events or forces that you cannot control. The solution to problems sometimes is inside you, not outside.

Key Takeaways

- *The secret of overcoming crisis is to look inside yourself deeply or your organization and focus with a goal of keeping the organization together or integrated.*
- *In other words, keep together and be integrated.*

You must also remember that you or the organization cannot control the forces coming from outside. External environmental forces cannot be stopped but have to be controlled or managed. Sometimes, crisis requires that we ask tough questions. What is wrong with me? What can I do? What resources do I have? What opportunities are available? Never ask, however, what is wrong with the world.

2. Management

Another approach that crisis will demand is management. What is management? Management is simply working with others to achieve goals. Management involves organizing and coordinating all actions or activities so that objectives that have been set are achieved. You must set goals, especially during any crisis. What is your goal or objective during a crisis? You need to think of the goals for your company or family or personal goals. Your goal could be any of the following:

- To survive and thrive.
- To ensure the organizational success.
- To avoid conflict.
- To avoid losing confidence from customers, clients or stakeholder.

To manage effectively, you will require quality and experienced managers. You need to learn management and apply the management ideas, concepts and knowledge. A lot of people struggle in life because they have never bothered to learn the concepts of management and leadership. Every crisis will require managers and leaders. The two concepts go together.

How Strong Are You?

Can you answer that question? How do you know that you are strong? You only know that you are strong because you can lift something? If I want to know that you are strong, then I will give you something to lift. Lifting implies I will be testing your strength. If you are able to lift something, then we can say you are really strong. If you cannot lift, push, or even pull something then our conclusion is that you are weak. If you prove your strength in lifting something, then we can believe that you are really strong. That means we shall have faith in you. In times of crisis, you need faith. Faith will help you stay strong. Your belief system will carry you through even the toughest times. It does not mean the crisis will go away, but you need faith to help you through it. The strength of your faith will determine how you will survive a crisis.

"Daniel in the Den of Lions" was a Crisis

Daniel is recorded and remembered in history because of a crisis. Daniel's story is documented in the Daniel 6. He was a faithful guy. He prayed three times a day. He believed in God. He was obedient to God. Nevertheless, God allowed Daniel to go into the den of a lion. Did Daniel expect to go to the lion's den? I believe like most of us that he had no expectation. He completely had no idea about what was going to happen. When he appeared in front of the rulers, he thought maybe they will kill him or take him to jail, but instead, they took him and three others in the lions' den. That to me was a crisis. As I said earlier, a crisis is something that happens to you that you do not expect. It is what I call an unexpected change. Daniel is like most of us on earth. We talk big. I have my God. I know God. I believe in God. But the God that we serve does not protect us from a crisis. God allows us to go throw crises, so we can put our faith in God. Daniel could not save himself from the crisis, but God knew about the crisis. He allowed it to prove that He is God. Remember this point: The strength of your faith can take you through hard times. Hard times are a manifestation of a crisis. Crisis always brings hard life experiences.

All Great Men and Women in History Have Encountered Crises

Think about that for a few minutes. If you study the records of all great men and women that appear in history books in which we refer to today, you will notice at some point in their lifetimes, they encountered crisis. Let us begin with some names. For example, Martin Luther King, Jr., he faced a crisis of fighting against oppression; he desired equality in civil right. Civil Rights movement was a big crisis in the United States of America.

Nelson Mandela, on the other hand, was imprisoned. That was a crisis. He never expected to go to jail for over 25 years. In another example, Yoweri Museveni, the Ugandan leader, went into exile. That was a crisis. The family had to fly to Sweden; it was a crisis. Donald Trump became bankrupt; that was a crisis. All great people in history in my view have encountered a crisis at some point in their lives.

Let us turn to the Biblical examples. Sarah was a barren woman; she encountered a crisis of having no child of her own. Abraham was childless for a long time, but Sarah and his faith kept them through the times of crisis. David found himself confronting Goliath, which was an unexpected crisis. Samson became blind, which was another crisis. Jacob stole his brother's right. He was a thief. We know all these people because of the things that happened to them. They went through a crisis. They came out of them. They managed crises properly.

For what are you known? From what crises have you emerged? I learned over 10 years ago that the key principle in life is to expect the best to come but prepare for the worst. You should learn to expect the best but get prepared for the worst. The worst will be a crisis. It will affect you. To overcome a crisis, you will need faith. It is the faith of these great Bible leaders that kept them strong. You need to develop strong faith. Strong faith is the faith that is developed through tests and perseverance. It is based on your knowledge of God and not the miracles or the things done by God. Strong faith is manifested in times of crisis. It is your only confidence. If you lose faith, you lost your confidence. What's next? You lose balance, stability, direction and the forces of life will crush your life or run over you.

God's Original Plan on Management

When God created the universe, He never allowed the rain to fall. He never allowed water to come in the Garden of Eden because He had not created a human being to manage the land. If you read Genesis 1 and 2, you will notice that Genesis 1 is a summary but Genesis 2 gives details of what happened in relation to the creation of man and the events that occurred in the Garden of Eden. God did not allow plants to grow because there was nobody to take care of the plants in the Garden. He wanted someone who was just like Him, in His own image. My question is this: God created man to do what?

Genesis 2 provides the answer:

This is the account of the heavens and the earth when they were created, when the LORD God made the earth and the heavens. Now no shrub had yet appeared on the earth and no plant had yet sprung up, for the LORD God had not sent rain on the earth and there was no one to work the ground, but streams came up from the earth and watered the whole surface of the ground. Then the LORD God formed a man from the dust of the ground and breathed into his nostrils the breath of life, and the man became a living being. Now the LORD God had planted a garden in the east, in Eden; and there he put the man he had formed. The LORD God made all kinds of trees grow out of the ground—trees that were pleasing to the eye and good for food. In the middle of the garden were the tree of life and the tree of the knowledge of good and evil. (Genesis 2: 4-8)

God never allowed plants to grow because man was not there to work the ground. What does working the ground imply? When you are working, it means you are responsible and you are expected to manage. You also reap and sow. God wanted human beings who were like Him to manage the Garden of Eden. He wanted responsible people. He never wanted careless managers and leaders. The Garden of Eden was a home for Adam and his family. But water came, according to the text in Genesis 2:8-15. God provided clear instructions to the people he created in His image:

Then God blessed them, and God said to them, "Be fruitful and multiply; fill the earth and subdue it; have dominion over the fish of the sea, over the birds of the air, and over every living thing that moves on the earth." And God said, "See, I have given you every herb that yields seed which is on the face of all the earth, and every tree whose fruit yields seed; to you it shall be for food. Also, to every beast of the earth, to every bird of the air, and to everything that creeps on the earth, in which there is life, I have given every green herb for food"; and it was so. Then God saw everything that He had made, and indeed it was very good. So the evening and the morning were the sixth day. (Genesis 1:28-31)

In my search for answers to life's questions, I have concluded that God's purpose of creating humans is found in the scripture above. Look at the words God uses:
Be fruitful, which means there is a seed somewhere in man and woman. Increase, which means multiply.

- Subdue the Earth.
- Rule over it.
- God gave man the choice to decide what happens on Earth.
- God gave man control over his destiny and everything on Earth.
- God gave man the power of will to mankind because we carry his moral nature, image or likeness.

There is something that I believe happened to Adam. I believe he encountered a crisis. You will recall that God created him and placed him in the Garden of Eden. God made him to be in charge of resources, wealth and everything else in the garden. I believe he enjoyed his time in the garden.

However, when God was disappointed by the disobedience, Adam was chased away from the garden (Genesis 3). Adam lost everything that God had given him for his life. He could not keep it. I believe that this is a good lesson to all of us on Earth. Sometimes God can give some things but you can lose them.

I figured it out years back in this way: everything that I have I will lose it one day. If I have a job, I will not have it forever. Why? There is nothing permanent. My own life will not be there forever. I will die one day. Maybe even my spouse, children or friends will go away or pass away. The only permanent thing on earth is God. What then do we need to do? We need to have faith in God who is permanent. We should take away our faith from temporary things including idols. We should not believe in temporary things or possessions. I need to prepare and get used to the fact or idea that temporary things will go away. My parents and grandparents are no longer with us. How things used to be 10 years ago is not what I see today. Some of my friends are gone or we are no longer in contact or even communicate. I recall we had them as a wonderful blessing. They gave us opportunities, love and protected us from famine, diseases and other problems.

An example that I recall is how much we prayed for grandmother, but she left to be with God. I prayed. I fasted for her. I believe she finished to do the work God created her to do or completed her assignment. When you do not know what to do, you need to trust God. I recall even my own late father, I called friends to pray with us. Some fasted, but God decided the destiny of his life.

When I tell you that everything you have you will lose, it is not a negative prophesy. It is the truth. I recall King David saying that some trusted in chariots but he will trust in the name of our Lord God. Why would a king take away his trust from chariots or swords? Because chariots or swords are temporary. Only God is permanent. David had his faith in God. He trusted God in all life. He knew that with God, he would still win. You will win only if you trust God. No matter the level of crisis, you will win if you trust God. Your faith should never be in people. Take your faith away from people. Your faith should be in God (Mark 11:22). Your faith should never be in people.

Let me explain a little. There are people or folks who will disappoint you or sometime in your life. They will not hold the promises or commitment they have given you or to the organization. If you trust make promises and commitments, they will abandon you. They might not even walk with you in your crisis. They will abandon you. Get ready on your own to manage any crisis that comes around.

What to Do in Times of Crisis

During the times of crisis, you should become fruitful, have an increase, rule the world, etc. God's intention for man's creation was rulership. He wanted a ruler. The intent was to set up a Kingdom on earth ruled by man. When Adam failed in management of the Garden of Eden, God threw him out and everything changed. Adam must have encountered a crisis. He was used to getting free food, but God said you have to work for it now and sweat. God decided to change the conditions in the Garden of Eden. Why? Because the manager or the ruler failed to dominate or rule it. To me the greatest lesson of life is management. I always say a simple statement that goes like this: Everything or whatever you mismanage, you will lose it.

The Truth About Mismanagement

- If you mismanage your relationships, you will not keep them.
- If you mismanage your money, you will lose it.
- If you mismanage your life, it will be gone.
- If you mismanage your marriage, you will see what happens.
- If you mismanage your organization or corporation, the outcome is known already.
- If you mismanage your resources, you will lose the resources.
- If you misuse your assets, you will end up in debt or liabilities; you will lose.
- If you mismanage your job, you will not keep it.
- If you violate laws, you will be affected at some point in time.
- Anything that you mismanage, you will lose it!

Mismanagement is the Source of World Problems

Most of all the problems in the world are a result of mismanagement. Check what is happening in your city or country. You will find that only a fraction of people, less than 5 percent in some cases, are good managers. The remaining 95 percent are bad managers. They have gifts that they have failed to manage. For instance, God gave Adam to be in charge of the gift called the Earth. He was irresponsible. He blamed the woman. He mismanaged it. You know the outcomes: sweat, pain and hard work. How do I know that God gave man the Earth? Psalms 115: 15-16 says, "May you be blessed by the Lord, the Marker of Heaven and Earth. The highest heaven belongs to the Lord, but the earth He has given to man." What has man done as regards the earth? Mismanaged it! All environmental problems are a result of mismanagement. Corporations are closing down causing crises to individuals, families or nations because of mismanagement.

How Does Mismanagement Come About And How Does It Cause a Crisis?

I want to challenge you to think. My perspective of this is as follows. I believe mismanagement is a result of irresponsibility. I believe it is a result of rebellion. It is caused by disregard of laws. You should be wondering how. Let us use an example. Suppose you are the decision maker of an organization or corporation, and the founders of the organization have established all laws or policies that all members must follow in executing their duties. Suppose you are in charge of the finance department. You disregard the financial policies; you will find that the funds in the organization might run out.

If you ignore policies and do things on your own way, it means you are no longer following the laws established. You have become irresponsible. Very soon, the organization will be in chaos. Stakeholders will not enjoy the benefits that come from association with the organization. You see, a crisis will hit the organization because you mismanaged the funds and ignored the laws. Never tamper with laws. Be careful to keep the laws because laws enable good management. It is also biblical.

3. Preserve and Protect Your Culture in Crisis Times

A crisis can cause cultures to be buried and forgotten. Culture is a source of values, norms and beliefs that societies live by. Culture help maintains order and dignity. Culture guide societies. In the start of our discourse on crises, I listed the various effects of crises. You can see all that in Chapter 1. If you do not have time to see, let me mention them again—trauma, fear, depression, chaos, frustration, despair, anxiety, hopelessness, sadness, loss of morals, wailing, weeping, worrying and many others conditions. Crises erode cultures and destroy values. Think about this for a second.

Let me explain something. I recall during the war in Northern Uganda during the late 1990's, a lot people (estimated to over 3 million people) were forced to live in camps. Life became horrible. Families disintegrated. So many challenges were faced; women and girls engaged in prostitution. I do not blame them. It was a result of change in human conditions. They were uprooted from their homes or places of origin and forced to live in camps. What happened? Values were lost. When values are lost, culture gets affected.

Another example I am familiar with is from Somalia. War has ravaged that country since 1991 when the government disintegrated and fell apart. The Somalis have a rich culture, but they have struggled to keep it. You will go to any part of the world; you will get Somalis living together in one community. Why? I think they are preserving their culture. Crisis has caused them to go live in exile, but believe me they are together in exile with their culture living in one community. If you go to Kenya, you will get a majority of Somalis in Eastlighee. Anywhere in the world, you will find those beautiful people living in one community.

4. Storing and Saving Resources

There is a story that I think of each time there is a report of famine in the world. Famine is not new. But when it happens, it becomes a crisis. It causes loss of lives and many adverse effects. Joseph, who was sold by his brothers to Egyptian merchants, was made to be in-charge of planning against the famine that affected Egypt. Famine is a crisis. During famine, people die, and property are lost, including livestock.

Do you know what Joseph did? He stored and saved the food (grains) that was obtained during a bumpy harvest season. The grains were kept for the period of scarcity and respond to a potential crisis of famine. To survive a crisis, you must store and save some of your resources for the future. I have been involved with the United Nation in humanitarian crises. This is what they call it. They call it "contingency planning and preparedness." Develop a contingency plan and be prepared for a crisis. It is important for you as a manager and leader to create an emergency plan. This sounds so simple but it is very critical. Furthermore, Joseph shows us that proper management is critical. He also shows us the importance of resource management. A person's resources protect them from crisis. You must therefore ensure that you develop a saving culture.

In my culture, as an Etesot from Eastern Uganda, we used to have granaries, used as stores of food after the harvest season. Food was always stored in the granaries. I recall my grandparents had over 20 granaries for food in the compound. During the dry season, I would see them get food and use it. The same can be said for green vegetables, which would be used as a buffer for the dry season. All of these practices were meant to prepare families for the difficult seasons of life. I believe even effective governments must develop an initiative of saving critical resources to save the populations that might be impacted by crisis. For instance, effective government leaders must have fuel or oil reserves; they must have grain stores for food especially cereals and pulses.

Further, they must have trained personnel to deal with emergencies. Aside from that, they should also have funds set aside for emergencies or disasters. Emergency funds must be available for immediate response and timely action to avert the impact of crisis on people.

5. Develop and Manage Trustful Relationships

When I was growing up as a teenager, I used to read my Good News Bible all through. There is a story of trust in the bible. I love the way it is said in Luke 16, The Parable of the Dishonest Steward:

Then he also said to his disciples, "A rich man had a steward who was reported to him for squandering his property. He summoned him and said, 'What is this I hear about you? Prepare a full account of your stewardship, because you can no longer be my steward.' The steward said to himself, 'What shall I do, now that my master is taking the position of steward away from me?

I am not strong enough to dig and I am ashamed to beg. I know what I shall do so that, when I am removed from the stewardship, they may welcome me into their homes.' He called in his master's debtors one by one. To the first he said, 'How much do you owe my master?' He replied, 'One hundred measures of olive oil.' He said to him, 'Here is your promissory note. Sit down and quickly write one for fifty.' Then to another he said, 'And you, how much do you owe?' He replied, 'One hundred kors of wheat.' He said to him, 'Here is your promissory note; write one for eighty.' And the master commended that dishonest steward for acting prudently."
(Luke 16: 1-8)

Application of the Parable

For the children of this world are more prudent in dealing with their own generation than are the children of light. I tell you, make friends for yourselves with dishonest wealth, so that when it fails, you will be welcomed into eternal dwellings. The person who is trustworthy in very small matters is also trustworthy in great ones; and the person who is dishonest in very small matters is also dishonest in great ones. If, therefore, you are not trustworthy with dishonest wealth, who will trust you with true wealth? If you are not trustworthy with what belongs to another, who will give you what is yours? No servant can serve two masters. He will either hate one and love the other, or be devoted to one and despise the other. You cannot serve God and mammon. (Luke 16: 1-8)

In that story, you see that Jesus commended and appreciated the efforts of two servants but the master fired the servant who wasted the master property without investing it. Resources need to be well managed.

The Critical Lessons from the Parable

- If you mismanage little things, you will also mismanage big things.
- If you are trustworthy in very small matters, you will also be trustworthy in great ones.
- If a person is dishonest in very small matters, that person will also be dishonest in great ones.
- If, therefore, you are not trustworthy with wealth, who will trust you with true wealth?
- Crisis can happen because there are people who are dishonest living among us.
- Focus in major things is important for effective leadership.

6. Value Addition

Everything that is done, there must be a willingness to add value. Value addition is important during crisis. If you are going to overcome crisis, you must pursue the direction of value addition. You need to engage in continuous increase of value. Let me give an example. If you are going to be downsized in your job, it means you are not valuable anymore. But if you have been involved in value addition, you cannot be downsized easily. A crisis of a job loss can be caused by the reduction of your value. Do you see my point here? How do you add value? There are many ways to do it. My answer is management. How do I mean?

- You need to be effective.
- You need to become efficient.
- You need to have correct and right attitudes.
- You need to use resources appropriately.
- You need to carry out planning and determine what you need to do.

Let us refresh our memories. What is management? To me management is the efficient, effective, proper and timely use of resources entrusted to you and aimed at increasing productivity and adding value.

Questions for You to Ponder

- How have you added value to yourself?
- Does the organization have value needed in the marketplace or meet the needs of stakeholders?
- What value do you bring to your job or organization?
- What is value addition to you?
- How are you efficient?
- How are you effective?
- Do you use your resources properly?
- Are you managing your time effectively?

7. Exploit and Use Your Talents and Resources at Hand

In times of crisis, people with skills and knowledge will be required. If you have a talent, it even gets better. You cannot buy talents. You are born with it. You cannot borrow it. But talents can be developed and used. If you develop and use your talents, it will open opportunities. Remember, crisis not only comes with adversity but also with opportunities. You might have read a story of talents in the Bible. You can refer to Matthew 25:14-30. Two guys received money and they increased it. They added value to the money they received from their master. But one of the guys did nothing with money. He decided to bury the money and when the master learned about that, he was scolded and abused. He lost the money too. Can I say this? His talent was taken away! In reality, the guy never added value to what he received. When you receive something, add value. When you get first degree, add value. When you get cows, add value. Anything to which you add value will save you from a potential crisis.

In that story, the master (manager or leader) used a kind of language that I consider very strong. He described the guy as "wicked but also lazy." "You wicked, lazy servant, you should have put my money on deposit with bankers, so that I could get interest." (Matthew 25: 26-27). When you get interest, you have added value to the original money. What does it mean by being wicked? What is wickedness? According to Jesus, wickedness means irresponsibility. It may also mean mismanagement. It could mean an inability to add value. It also takes resources entrusted to you and cause them to lose value. I believe, that majority of people are wicked in their own way. In my life, I have always tried to avoid being labeled "wicked and lazy."

Let me remind you of an interesting experience when Moses, the leader of Israel, had a crisis of crossing the Red Sea with over a million people. For purposes of reference, you can study it in the book of Exodus 4:2-6. When Moses had reached a point where Egyptians were pursuing the Israelites to take them back as slaves, Moses the leader had a big problem to cross over the sea. What happened? God asked Moses at the time of a crisis, what he had.

Moses replied he had a staff. Then the Lord told Moses to throw it on the ground. Moses did as God instructed him and it became a snake. Moses was scared; he actually ran away from the stick that turned into the snake. God instructed Moses to reach out and the snake became the original staff he had before God's instructions. Moses used the staff to overcome a crisis. If they had not crossed the sea, probably, the enemy would have arrested or killed them. Who knows? What saved them were the resources available at hand.

What do you have as resources? Use those resources to save yourself from a crisis. What business ideas do you have? Develop a business idea and turn it into products and services. You will find people paying for the product or service. What talents do you have? Have you been developing your talents? Are your talents dormant?

What Are Some Actions That You Need to Take Here?

- Add value to yourself. Increase your value.
- Add value to how you use the time you have.
- Become creative and innovative.
- Add value to the friendships (personal and professional).
- Think of strategies for value addition in business, education, health, investments, assets, etc.

8. Work Hard

Crisis will demand that you or your organization work even harder. You might have heard the saying "Hard work pays." This is very true. Lazy people always have excuses. To avoid getting caught up in a crisis, sometimes you need to work hard or even harder. Do not spend time complaining about work or how hard it is. Do not avoid work. When you work hard, it will pay you in the end. King Solomon wrote the words, "Lazy hands make a man poor, but diligent hands bring wealth" (Proverbs 10:4). The choice is in your hands. You are responsible for your future and destiny. You either work hard and get paid or be lazy and experience the effects of poverty. I was there as a teenager. I lived a miserable life. I had no shoes or clothes. I slept on dirty floor and when I read the wisdom of King Solomon, I decided to work hard.

The opposite of laziness is diligence. The opposite of poverty is wealth. What do you want to be? What is your choice? Every time I meet a person who is lazy, I notice they do not possess the quality of diligence. A diligent person is also a patient individual or person. These two attributes are very critical and should not be separated. An individual who has those qualities has a good character. If diligent and patient people work hard, they will produce desired results. They can achieve anything. A patient and diligent person has the potential of being an effective manager. They are capable of bringing value or adding values.

Practical Actions to Overcome Poverty And Attract Wealth

- Explore ways to overcome bad habits such as laziness.
- Exploit your potential.
- Learn how to become an effective manager.
- Find ways to bring and add value to your business, career, or organization.

The Life After Makerere University

I remember when I left Makerere University, I had no idea of where I was going. I never had relatives that would connect me to a job. However, as I walked out of the university, I decided that I was going to work hard and exercise diligence. I knew the outcome would be wealth and prosperity. I knew I would defeat poverty and acquire some assets and lay a strong foundation for my family. I remember, unemployment was one of the major crisis which I faced. Life was tough but the tough times never destroyed my faith and confidence in God. One of the lessons, I learned during the times of unemployment, which a crisis was patience. During times of crisis, I also learned the need for faith, endurance and patience. Today, I have acquired a few assets, which were not there when I started. I also live a life according to my own ability.

However, one of the sad reality is that some people perceive crisis as a bad thing. If you are facing any crisis, I would like to consider it as a blessing and opportunity. I remember some of my friends from University who never encountered the unemployment crisis. When they left the gates of Makerere University, they immediately were offered jobs in government and large organizations. The irony is that the never learned anything from a crisis. When, they lost those opportunities, some of them never recovered.

The book of Proverbs has a lot of information about laziness and diligence. For instance, Proverbs 13:4 says, "The appetite of the sluggard craves but has nothing, but the appetite of the diligent is amply satisfied." People whom King Solomon calls sluggards are lazy people. They never want to work hard. They are impatient.

They expect miracles. They want to get luck. They never think of the value of hard work. They avoid work. They waste time in useless ventures and things. However, "The plans of the diligent lead to profit as surely as haste leads to poverty." (Proverbs 21:5) It is up to you and it all depends on your choices and decisions.

9. Maximize Your Faith During Crisis

The times of crisis can mean to tough times. They can be hard times. There can be dark nights and you do not see the light at the end of the tunnel. Sometimes, nights can be longer than days, days longer than weeks, months than years. The crisis makes you restless or helpless. What you expected turns out to be the unexpected. What do you in such a situation?

What do you need most in crisis? If you are a Christian or religious person, I believe you need faith. To do what? To help you go through the crisis. If you lose faith, a crisis will destroy you. Here is what I mean...

I have come to know that life is a mysterious experience. It is full of mysteries that man cannot even explain. Scientists might try to explain certain things, but they will give you half the story. Things happen when you do not expect and they affect you. When things happen unexpectedly, what do you do? How do you respond? Unexpected occurrences change but also a crisis. A crisis is a result of unexpected change as well as changes from normal to abnormal states of things.

Think and consider the truth below:

- There are things in life that you will not be able to control.
- There are things in life that you cannot stop.
- There are things in life that you cannot explain.
- There are things in life that you are not responsible for.
- There are things in life that you cannot change.
- There are things in life that you cannot exceed or go beyond.
- There are things in life that will happen to you unexpected.

When I was a teenager, I used to go to graveyard where my mother and grandparents were buried. I would sit there for the whole day. Those moments of self-reflection and loneliness taught me the statements above. I learned I could not bring back my relatives to life. I could not change what happened to them. I learned that I could not even control or stop death. I recall my grandmother, whom I miss so dearly. She fell sick and I used to care for her. I tried my best to go to the hospital and assist her with her medications and in general. In the end, we lost her. That taught me life lessons that would become a guide to my earthly journey. I had to accept the facts that it happened. There is one thing I need to say: All of us will die one day. You need to clear that from your mind.

What do you do in such a situation as I have described above? I found the secrets. I will share them here. First, you need to know that a crisis is an event. It will happen only for a season. It will not last forever. God loves us so much that He says in His word:

"There is an appointed time for everything and a time for every affair under the heavens" (Ecclesiastes 3:1). But I like what the NKJV says: *"To everything there is a season, a time for every purpose under heaven."*

The scripture above teaches me that everything in life has a season. Seasons are not permanent. Seasons come and go. There are four seasons in the western world: winter, spring, summer and fall. Change in seasons can bring a crisis. To live effectively, you must have faith that when a season changes, a new season will come again. So many things always change. There is a season for crisis and a season for living without a crisis. Even relationships and partnerships go through seasons. You never engage in things that can destroy you when a season passes and because of crisis. For instance, you never throw away your summer clothes when the season ends. You keep the clothes because there will be another season of summer. A crisis is often caused by unexpected change. You get disappointed because you never expected your spouse to change. If you want to avoid or minimize the disappointments, you must also lower the level of expectations.

Furthermore, crisis forces you to look at the past and how things used to be. Maybe you had a good family and now your family members have died in a plane crash. Maybe terrorists killed your family members or something happened. What do you do? You can cry but not forever. You need to accept what has happened and forget about it. I like what Paul said: "Forget what lies behind and pressing towards the goal."

However, before we look at another approach to overcoming crisis, let me say somethings for you to know:

- There are things in life that only God knows.
- There are things in life that only God understands.
- There are things in life that only God can change.
- There are things in life that only God can stop.
- There are things in life that only God can control.
- There are things in life that you can never explain. They will always be a mystery.
- There are things that exceed you. You have limitations. Your capacity is limited.
- Your limitations can be your strength in crisis and keeps you peaceful.
- Learn to manage the unexpected when it comes.

With that in mind, what then should be our response? Let me give you my thoughts:

- Somethings will always remain a mystery.
- Somethings only God understands.
- Somethings only God knows.
- Somethings only God can stop.
- Somethings only God can change.
- Somethings only God can control.
- Somethings only God can explain.
- Somethings are God's responsibility.

If you have these concepts with you in times of crisis, you will have a different attitude even you have lost your house or shop when it burned down and all your lifetime energy, effort and resources have been destroyed in 30 minutes or 3 hours. You will have peace and a winner's attitude.

10. Forget Some Things

There are some things that you have to forget. Life will change and you must forget the past. If you keep remembering what used to happen or the way things used to be, you will always be depressed. How life used to be will get you worried and under unnecessary pressure. You will die early and so will your organization. You will also weep and wail. The words of the Apostle Paul resonate very well here. He said words that will help you focus on the future and the goal. In times of crisis, your goal is to stay alive or save your organizational life.

Here is what Paul said to the Philippians:

Not that I have already attained, or am already perfected; but I press on, that I may lay hold of that for which Christ Jesus has also laid hold of me. Brethren, I do not count myself to have apprehended; but one thing I do, forgetting those things which are behind and reaching forward to those things which are ahead, I press toward the goal for the prize of the upward call of God in Christ Jesus. Therefore, let us, as many as are mature, have this mind; and if in anything you think otherwise, God will reveal even this to you. (Philippians 3: 12-14)

Paul was persecuted, but instead of looking at the events that happened in his journey, he had a different attitude. He was focused on the goal and the future. He was never concerned with the past. Why? Because he could not change what happened in the past. My question to you is: Do you have power to change events of the past? Can you change the past? Remember, I said that there are things you cannot change. The past is one of them. Always remember the past cannot be changed, but you can plan your future. Your future depends on the goals that you set to achieve. You must have a goal. That goal will keep you strong even when things are going bad. Because goals give you hope and an imagination about the positive and exciting future that is coming into view.

You also need to exercise maturity in the different areas of your life. Paul talks of maturity as a way to forget the past. Maturity is your ability to maintain your balance even when things are not going on well. Maturity is about being able to maintain personal balance amidst chaos and tragedy. People who are mature never panic during times of crisis, but they plan. They never allow pressure to oppress them, but they believe in their purpose and vision. They are also aware that problems are temporary. No problem is permanent. You should forget the past but focus on the future and your critical goals. Learn to forget some things so that you will have peace. The weight of the past is always dangerous. It pulls you back. It stops you from moving forward. When you keep remembering the past, the past will make you powerless and your future becomes distant. The power of the future is not trapped in the past. It is available when you focus your energy and effort to change what has gone wrong to create a better and prosperous future. Use the power of the future to overcome past failures, mistakes, problems and challenges.

11. Live by Faith: Combine Your Faith with Work

In crisis times, you need to live by faith. Apostle Paul wrote to the Romans these words:

"Who shall separate us from the love of Christ? Shall tribulation, or distress, or persecution, or famine, or nakedness, or peril, or sword? As it is written: "For Your sake we are killed all day long; we are accounted as sheep for the slaughter." Yet in all these things we are more than conquerors through Him who loved us. For I am persuaded that neither death nor life, nor angels nor principalities nor powers, nor things present nor things to come, nor height nor depth, nor any other created thing, shall be able to separate us from the love of God which is in Christ Jesus our Lord." (Romans 8:35-40)

Look at this message. Do you know the context when Paul wrote these words? Paul was in jail. Jail is not a nice place. Look at Paul's attitude. Paul was convicted that God's love was far greater than any crisis. How about you? Where is your faith? Faith alone is not sufficient. You also need to combine faith with work. For your faith to produce any results, you must work, but without any effort, the faith you possess is a dead faith.

Also, what is faith? Faith is not difficult to define. Faith is belief. Faith is your confidence in life. Without faith, you will lose your confidence. You will begin to have negative thoughts and fear will set in. You will wail. You will weep. You will also worry a lot. The writer of Hebrews gives the definition that I believe you need to put into your heart and remember it for the rest of your life. Let me quote it for: *"Now faith is the substance of things hoped for, the evidence of things not seen."* (Hebrews 11:1)

Sometimes you will never understand what is happening or why the crisis happened. You will need faith to take you through hard times. You cannot survive a crisis without faith. Just remember that things you hope to achieve will happen because of faith in God (Mark 11:22). You need to have faith in God. Never have faith in things that will go away in the morning or tomorrow. You need to remember that all things will change, except God.

Why do we trust God? What makes you believe in God? What makes you have confidence in God? Because God never changes. He is the same yesterday, today and forever. What about humans around you? Are they like God? No. They are just humans. They will change as time passes. They might even disappoint you. They might even turn against you. You might become enemies or friends. Faith saved the Hebrew boy named Daniel from the Den of Lions. Faith saved three Hebrew folks from the furnace. What crisis are you facing right now? Your faith will bring you out that situation.

12. Use A Crisis as an Opportunity to Thrive

The impact of a crisis on individuals, families, communities, organization and nations can be overwhelming. If you are going to survive a crisis, you must view it as an opportunity. What is an opportunity? An opportunity refers to something that you can exploit based a given set of circumstances where the outcomes are uncertain but require the resources to be committed even when you or the organization can be exposed to risks. There will always be risks in life.

Further, a crisis will expose you to risks but you need to exploit the situation for your advantage and benefit. I recall a situation when I was facing a crisis of an impending job loss; I was not ready and my contract was ending. I was facing an unexpected situation. I did not know what to do. I looked the opportunities that were coming as a result of the crisis. I decided I would use my time very well, carry out major restructuring, and minimize wastage of other resources. That crisis enabled me to become a better planner and increased my level of focus and discipline. I developed my personal level of discipline. That discipline enabled me to accomplish the writing of this book.

Therefore, you should look at a crisis as something that will benefit you or your organization. I recall also in Northern Uganda during the Lord Resistance Army war against the government of Uganda from 2002-2007: it was a difficult time. One thing that amazed me was that many businesses emerged and millionaires were borne out of that crisis. The crisis turned into an opportunity. Crisis has been said to be "a mother of invention."

13. Be Fruitful, Multiply and Subdue

We find these words mentioned by God to man who He created in His image. In fact, see what God said: *"Then God blessed them, and God said to them, 'Be fruitful and multiply; fill the earth and subdue it; have dominion over the fish of the sea, over the birds of the air, and over every living thing that moves on the earth."* (Genesis 1: 28) How can God instruct mankind to be fruitful? Fruitful means to be full of fruits. Remember it is impossible to be fruitful without having a seed. Then He says multiply? To multiply what? Multiply what you have-fruits.

Further, God says fill the earth, subdue, and dominate. Let me explain what fruitful means in Hebrew: it means to be productive. Multiply means to reproduce what you have produced based on your productive process and activities. To dominate means to rule the earth with your products from the multiplication process. God did not create you without a seed. He placed a seed inside of you. That seed will produce fruits and when you are full of fruits, you will multiply and dominate your environment.

In times of crisis, you need to identify the seed that you have. What is your gift? What are you able to produce as a fruit and then multiply? If you have a talent, you need to use it in times of crises. A lot of people never have an idea of their seed or gift. Think of the gifts that you have; the gifts will save you out of a crisis. Maybe you are a tailor, carpenter, teacher or social worker, you need to show up with your gift. I recall watching a horrible story of Jewish prisoners under the hands of the Nazis in a movie called escape from Sobibor. People or prisoners were separated because of their gifts. They were received at the camp. Those who were taken to some place to use their skills, talents and gifts did not die immediately from the chambers. Whereas those who had no gifts were immediately taken to the chambers for what was called "the cleansing." They died immediately or were killed.

- What is your gift?
- What is your seed?
- What can you make to become a fruit?

14. Never Apply Permanent Solutions to Temporary Problems

Every problem or crisis is temporary. Temporary does not mean it will take a short time, but it may mean that it might even take years. One thing is certain: No problem is permanent unless it kills you or if you die. Problems are temporary. They come in seasons. They never last forever. There will be days that seem to take longer than nights. There will be nights that seem to take longer than days. There will be dry seasons that are longer than rainy seasons. There will be winter seasons that seem longer than summer.

However, none of the seasons will be last forever. Just as seasons are temporal, so are problems. You will not be poor forever. You will not mourn forever the loss of a loved one. You will not have a flood that last forever. The longest duration of flooding in history is forty days and forty nights. It ended.

How long is your situation? Do you think it will be forever? I do not think so. God says the following words in Genesis 8:22: *"For as long as the Earth lasts, planting and harvest, cold and heat, summer and winter, day and night will never stop."* What does God mean in the statement above? He means that as long

118

as we are living on earth, we are going to have time for planting but also harvest. The point is this: Planting will never be forever. Harvesting will also be for a short period. You might not get a good harvest, which means you might have a crisis of food or poor returns on your effort and hard work. To me, I believe that life is dictated by seasons.

Let me repeat something that you should not ever do with an example. Do not commit suicide when there is a crisis. Do not engage in activities that can destroy your life and the life of others. What I mean by this is that you should never apply a permanent solution to temporary problems. Problems will always be part of life as long as you are living on Earth. They are unavoidable. Get used to having problems. Get used to challenges and crises. As you get used to challenges, you will become immune or vaccinated against the problems.

If you are going to be a leader, get used to attacks, ridicule, and disagreements. You need to learn how to handle setbacks, disappointments, failures, frustrations and problems. Learn know how to manage and respond to problems. Everything in life is learned. You learn to walk, talk, sing, write, read and many other things. Everything is learned but people do not want to learn. Whose problem is that?

15. Seek Counselors for Support

A crisis often affects people in different ways. Others have the capacity to cope with it; it is called resilience or endurance. Others get broken down completely by it. For instance, you experience the loss of colleagues at work because they died in an automobile accident, or due to a terrorist attack, or gunned down innocently. These are all traumatic events that cause worry, doubts, fears, depression and hopelessness. You find yourself emotionally helpless and filled with grief and sad with darkness that does not go away at all.

In the year 2002, I was working in northern Uganda where Lord's Resistance Army had displaced several thousands of people. In addition, south Sudanese refugees were living in a settlement in one district called Pader, which part of Northern Uganda. It was a very difficult time. We had to deal with threats and security risks all the time and many times people would be ambushed, killed, attacked on the road, or camps. There were also rehabilitation centers in parts of northern Uganda. The centers were very helpful for assisting survivors. I recall even those providing services and support would become affected after repeated encounters and sights of sad events, death and victims.

However, what helped the situation was availability and extension of counseling services and assistance by counseling. The counselors did a great job to support survivors. Therefore, it is important to seek advice or help when you encounter a crisis. Go for counseling. Do not fear to ask for support. This is not about people anymore; it is about your health, life, future and destiny. Counseling will enable you to recover and overcome the trauma; learn how to identify the effects; and cope and advise other victims or people that need help. There are people who will always give wrong advice and who do not go for counseling because it shows you are not strong or you are weak. Ignore those people. Leave them alone. Everybody on earth needs help. Even powerful people and leaders all have advisors and personal doctors. They consult them when they need help. What makes you so special? You are a human being; if you care, you will likely be affected. Seek help when you can and get back on the road to achieve what God created you to do.

There was a story of a young man who I knew personally. He had a crisis of losing his job. The entire life of the young man depended on the job. When he lost the job, he decided to withdraw from the public and from his friends. He found solace in drugs and high consumption of alcohol. He was drunk day in and day out. Every day, he was busy drinking. He was depressed. He lost weight. Instead of looking at life in another perspective, he looked at life using the lenses of a failure. He saw himself as a failure. He viewed himself as unsuccessful and therefore useless on Earth. When life became unbearable. He wrote a chit, which said, "Bye. I have no reason to live." He killed himself. The police carried out an investigation into what killed the young man and concluded that it had nothing to with foul play. It was due to heavy consumption of alcohol and drugs. What a tragedy!

When you go for counseling, you will find people with similar stories. Remember, King Solomon said that there is nothing new under the sun. Everything that has happened on Earth before us will happen again. The global crisis was there in the 1930s; there was war in 1918 and in 1945. So many wars have occurred after those wars. What has been will be again. You are not alone in a crisis; there are millions of other beings suffering from the same kind of crisis you are in right now. Maybe you are unemployed;

just know there are thousands with the same problem like you. Maybe you are sick; remember that in hospitals, they have many patients whose conditions might even be worse than yours. No wonder that is why hospitals were built; otherwise, they would have closed them.

Finally, counseling does not mean you are weak. It means you value your future. What happens in life like the death of a loved one cannot be changed once it happens? The power you have is your future; you have not lived it. If you have a lost a job, there are probably better businesses and opportunities coming your way soon. Counseling means you are determined to have a better health and better perspectives so you can plan your unlived life in the future and enjoy the benefits of time. The passage of time also will help you to forget the past. You will realize the pain will start to fade away. Time will heal your wounds. Go for counseling when you need help.

Chapter Six

CHANGE IS CONSTANT! CRISES ARE SEASONAL

*"Education is the most powerful weapon
which you can use to change the world."*
~ Nelson Mandela

You Must Outlast the Season of Crises

There is nothing that is more powerful than knowledge. I do not know if you agree with my assertion, I will refer you to the conversation between Jesus and disciples. The knowledge of situations and issues will help you understand life and different kinds of situations. Jesus spoke to the disciples using parables in Matthew the following words concerning knowledge.

The disciples came to him and asked, "Why do you speak to the people in parables?" He replied, "Because the knowledge of the secrets of the kingdom of heaven has been given to you, but not to them. Whoever has will be given more, and they will have an abundance. Whoever does not have, even what they have will be taken from them. This is why I speak to them in parables: "Though seeing, they do not see; though hearing, they do not hear or understand. In them is fulfilled the prophecy of Isaiah: You will be ever hearing but never understanding; you will be ever seeing but never perceiving. (Matthew 13:10-14)

There are millions of people without knowledge. Things happen and they cannot interpret what is happening around them. They cannot interpret the consequences of political, economical, social, technological, environmental and legal events or forces affecting them. They are completely ignorant and uneducated. They lack knowledge and that lack of knowledge leads to their destruction. Further, God says in Hosea what causes destruction.

My people are destroyed from lack of knowledge. "Because you have rejected knowledge, I also reject you as my priests; because you have ignored the law of your God, I also will ignore your children. (Hosea 4:6)

In order to gain knowledge, you must study, seek knowledge and get information. It is a serious process which must be taken seriously. Knowledge protects people from destruction because life is a serious matter which should not be played or gambled with. To know about change, you need to be educated. Even understanding life, it requires education. Life in itself is full of mysteries. The mystery of life is one of the most important things that I got to know during the course of my journey on Earth. Early in my life, I got this revelation that everything has its time. King Solomon said those words and I believe they are applicable when we speak of change. It simply means that all things are seasonal. It does not matter where you are or where you live; life is seasonal.

In my birthplace of Uganda, we have two main seasons, dry season and rainy season. When the dry season passes, you see the rainy season. None of the seasons stays forever. When you go to the western world, they have four seasons, which are summer, autumn, winter and spring. Again, they come and go. Seasons come with their inherent blessings. Some seasons are good and some are bad. The seasons bring both positive and negative aspects. Some seasons come and the view of the environment becomes green, while others become brown or even white in the case of some parts of the world where there is snow.

Furthermore, seasons might change the temperature conditions. The temperature might become either hot or cold. At times, the conditions can become sunny, sandy, cloudy or dry. These are some of the characteristics of seasons. What then do you do in such situations where life is full of surprises? You have to remember that those are seasons. They are temporary. Your capacity to handle the season depends upon your understanding that seasons come and go. They are never permanent. Every nation or community, people always get excited when a season passes and another one comes. For instance, people might complain about dry season but rejoice when rainy season begins. People might be fearful of the winter season but be excited of the summer season. Life is that way. You will find some farmers happy when they have a bumper harvest but frustrated when the seasonal crops have failed as a result of draught or bad weather. Even fishermen have a season when they are able to conduct their fishing business and obtain massive returns and profits of their labor, but also there are seasons when their efforts never really pay off.

The life of human beings also seems to be like the seasons described above. There is a season when things seem to be going good and then another where life seems to be going in the wrong direction. There comes a season when harvest is plentiful and then another when harvest is miserable and poor. It also follows as if dry season will never end. Then suddenly, the rainy seasons come and you find farmers rejoicing. Again, when the rainy seasons continues for a long period, you will notice the complaints that people bring out.

Individuals will experience both good and bad times, which come just as seasons. You will have times when you up the sky or mountain, then you are happy. Then from the mountain, you will go deep in the valley. You will see that hope almost diminishes. You sense that seasons come and go if you have that ability to discern. There will be seasons of plenty and seasons of scarcity. There will be seasons of work that will be followed by seasons of rest or no activity. There will be seasons of calmness and seasons of chaos. Chaos can create crisis but also stability. Any sudden change can also create tension, anxiety, desperation or fear. People generally never like change. We like traditions. We like to maintain the status quo. This is basic human nature.

There are times when one season takes a long time to pass while there is another season that takes a short time. When the season takes a longer time to pass, we agonize a lot; sometimes we worry, wail, or weep. I believe the key in those moments when the season is taking a long time to pass is to **outlast the season**. Usually, you cannot outlast season without knowledge of seasons or how change happens. There is nothing on earth that is as permanent as change. You must become aware that change is constant. Change is inevitable.

If you have been through a storm in the last season, you need to know that the storm was preparing you for another storm that is coming your way. Every storm is a classroom for the next storms of life. Your capacity to manage the storm depends on the faith that you have in God. Your strength will be tested during the times of crisis. Your survival will depend on the faith you have. How strong are you? The test will reveal your strength. Sometimes, God brings tests to check out how strong we are and how deep is our faith in him. Job is a perfect example of a person with strong and deep faith. (Job 1)

The Power of Outlasting Seasons of Crisis

In the western world, they have four seasons commonly known as winter, spring, summer, fall and autumn. The seasons mark the changes in time. Life changes when a new season arrives. A season divides the year such that there is different weather, daylight, rain or sunshine. For instance, during the fall, this is when the leaves fall of from trees. During the spring, you see some different weather. Why do seasons come? Can you stop seasons? Seasons indicate that nothing is constant or permanent. Each season requires a different response. For instance, you could be using light clothes when it is summer and heavy clothes when it is winter. Life is that way. When seasons change, you need to change; otherwise, you will be destroyed.

Seasons are natural occurrences that nobody has the power to make happen. No government can dictate and direct that winter season go away so that there will be another season. No government or powerful individual can stop the dry season. Seasons come by themselves. Seasons come and go. A lot people on Earth do not like change. But seasons are an indicator of change. When seasons come, it means something is changing. Change is happening. You cannot stop change.

However, if your organization understands the nature of seasons, you will also realize it comes with its own benefits. For instance, a rainy season might result in a bumpy harvest for farmers or a good business season for fishermen. A dry season might be good for traders who have kept their produce and sell them during the season when food is not available. What you consider as a bad season might be an opportunity for another person. Every season has its benefits that you must learn to appreciate. Seasons can bring storms.

The Power of Storms:

1. It cleans up the environment and you will see it as fresh and clear.
2. It removes weak structures, trees or even buildings.
3. It forces people to learn new ways to survive.
4. It forces people to go back to God.
5. It also reveals which structures or buildings have strong foundations.
6. It also makes people better prepared of future storms and its effects.

Have you ever encountered a storm? I recall in my own life the seasons when I had nothing - no money, job, food or even accommodation. Those moments were difficult moments. It was as if I was living in Hell on Earth. I recall we slept in bush for fear of Karamojong warriors who were armed cattle rustlers. They raided all our animals. There was a crisis. People were displaced. People were living like wild animals in the forests. We had no clothes. We had no food. We had no water. We had no toilets. We had no shelter. Mosquitoes and roaches were eating us. We had to run and hide in the bushes to avoid being captured. We had to climb trees during the day to observe from which direction they were coming from. That is a crisis. How did we manage it? We believed in God. I recall people praying for peace until God brought back peace.

However, those moments gave me the opportunity to develop my character, humility, perseverance, resilience, endurance and faith. Just imagine how good those things I have listed are! They were established and built because of change and seasons. I also recall the seasons of plenty such as having a good job, good income, good things and life. In those seasons, some things were not right because I got involved in buying things that were not necessary. Then another season of crisis comes where life takes a different turn bringing disappointments, threats of sickness, death isolation etc. In those moments, the only thing I recall having trust in God. I spend a lot of time praying and it developed my faith further along with providing me a better understanding of life.

Who Created Seasons?

Let me be straight here. No human being or powerful nation can create any seasons that I wrote about in the earlier part of this book. You will also recall that I said that seasons are natural. Seasons were created by God. God created days and nights, which become weeks, months, years, decades and centuries, etc. God created seasons in Genesis 1:14: *"Then God said, "Let there be lights in the firmament of the heavens to divide the day from the night; and let them be for signs and seasons, and for days and years."* Here is when God created seasons. Light, which is responsible for dividing or separating the day from the night, also allows the signs as well as seasons to come, which influence the arrival of days, nights, weeks, month and years.

King Solomon, the wisest king that ever lived and ruled, wrote:

To everything there is a season, A time for every purpose under heaven: A time to be born, And a time to die;
A time to plant, And a time to pluck what is planted;
A time to kill, And a time to heal;
A time to break down, And a time to build up;
A time to weep, And a time to laugh;
A time to mourn, And a time to dance;
A time to cast away stones, And a time to gather stones;
A time to embrace, And a time to refrain from embracing;
A time to gain, And a time to lose;
A time to keep, And a time to throw away;
A time to tear, And a time to sew;
A time to keep silence, And a time to speak;
A time to love, And a time to hate; A time of war,
And a time of peace. (Ecclesiastes 3:1-8)

Instead of using the word "time," you can use the word "season." Let us go back to the text. You will see that "time to die" is a crisis. The time to, "throw away" is a crisis. The, "time of war" is a crisis; "time to kill" is a crisis. You will also notice, after a time of war, the season that follows is peace; after tearing down, it is building up; after time of uprooting, the next season is planting. You will see the balance between events or seasons. After the dry season, you will experience rainy season. Nothing really lasts forever. Nothing remains the same. Everything will change. God is good because He gives us time to live our lives in seasons. God gave us time to live our lives in time. This guarantees new hope that nothing on Earth lasts forever. The times when people die or kill each other are not good times. War times are bad times. Wars bring crises. Remember, that God does not live in time. He lives outside of time. God lives in eternity.

If you are going through a hard time right now, just remember that it is just a season. It will pass away. If you are happy right now with your family or organization, remember that it is just a season. It will not last forever. If you have been promoted recently, remember that it is a season. If you are down right now, remember that it is a season. Solomon said everything has its time. Notice the words that he used: Everything. He never said some things: He said all things have their time (Ecclesiastes 3:1).

Only God Is Permanent; Everything Else is Temporary

I have come to understand life in such a way that everything changes and nothing is permanent. The Bible says; He is the same yesterday, today and forever (Hebrews 13:8). This statement is referring to God. You can therefore be able to tell how God will be after 5 or 10 years. He will be the same. You and I will change. We might die. We might become disabled. We might change in our values, character or beliefs. We might change our associations or friends. We might change the places where we live today. We might get new spouses. We might lose our business. In other words, everything will change. Only God does not change and whatever God promise will not change. If you are experiencing a crisis, just remember God does not change, but change will occur. It is guaranteed. God will never protect us from seasons. He allows us to pass through seasons to enjoy the benefits of seasons. God allows seasons to come so that there will be a change. Change can be either destructive or constructive. Constructive change or season brings hope, while the destructive change causes fear.

You might be experiencing a "dry" economic season right now, never despair. Just remember there will be a "rainy economic season". There will be a season when you will have plenty of money. I have been to seasons when I was going through a dry economic season. I recall I was working for the United Nations World Food Program; I was earning a salary with a lot of responsibility, taking care of a large family with limited income. It was a dry economic season. It did not last forever. You might be the same, whatever you are going through, will never or not last forever. There will be a season of poverty followed by a season of plenty. Dry seasons will not last forever. You will not cry forever. You will not weep forever. You will not be at war forever. Rainy seasons will also not last forever. A change will come. Remember this as long as you live. A change will come.

Having a job is just a season. Being unemployed is also a season. You might be employed, but remember there is a possibility of unemployment ahead. You might be having power, but remember a season will come when that power will be taken away. You might be healthy now, but there might be a season when you will experience poor health. You must always be aware of seasons and be willing to handle them. Do not panic when a new season comes in. Just learn to handle it. Some seasons require planting, whereas others require planning.

Surviving a Season of Crisis Requires Faith and Belief

You cannot go through a season without faith. You need faith to carry you through tough times. Faith will give you hope to outlast the season. Faith will inform you that the long nights will not last forever; there will be a day coming. Faith will keep you focused that at the end of the dark tunnel there will be light. You have faith that winter will not last forever. Therefore, you will need to keep closer to God to help you through seasons. Why? God is the creator of time and seasons. He knows the beginning of seasons. He also knows the ends of seasons. Even the dark moments or seasons of life will pass away. Your belief system or faith will carry you through those moments.

John, one of the apostles of Jesus Christ, wrote in 1 John 5:4, that," *For whatever is born of God overcomes the world. And this is the victory that has overcome the world—our faith.*"

What does it mean by overcome? What is victory? When do you have victory? It is our faith that helps us to attain any victory. In times of crisis, we need to overcome it by faith. It is your faith that keeps you strong. It will help inform how you decide on matters. It determines your future. Your faith or belief system is what helps you in times of crisis. Overcoming tests requires faith. How big is your faith? How big is your God? How strong is your belief system? How many tests are you willing to pass through? Are you ready for the tests of life? Tests usually reveal the strength of our faith and its size.

What Happens When You Change Your Life?

If you make critical decisions, you will be able to cause a change in your life. There are many things that can happen. But how can you make changes in your life? I believe it requires courage. You have to fight the fear that interferes with your future. If you cannot change, your life will not be easy to live. Sometimes it requires looking at your dreams. Sometimes it requires reconditioning of the mind or renewal of your mind. Apostle Paul in Romans 12: 2 admonishes the disciples to transform their lives through renewing of the mind. As you look to the future and crisis that affects. It, never allow any doubt to stop you. Your circumstances cannot determine everything. There are possibilities in life. You might have made mistakes, committed errors or deal with a crisis; you will need a change your mindset. Norman Vincent Pearle said these words *"change your thoughts and you will change your world."*

Nothing really changes until there is a change in your mind. You could change your clothes, location, friends or careers, but until you change your thoughts, you will remain the same. When there is change in your thoughts or ideas in your mind, you will begin to behave differently. When I started years ago, changing and protecting what I was putting in my mind, my life started to take a different direction and getting to my desired destiny. I started to think differently. I avoided some friends because their ideas were not what I wanted to hear. Your ideas determine your actions and behaviors. Your behaviors determine your future. Your future is influenced by information that you have accumulated and accepted over the years. When you believe that the information is correct, they become your beliefs that form the belief systems and determine your life's philosophy.

Furthermore, human beings are created with seeds on the inside. Think about that statement. That is why when you get an apple or mango seed, it has seeds on the inside. Because of that fact, I have the confidence that God places the future of everything in itself. The future of the seeds is placed inside. It is trapped inside. As you go through a crisis, you need to remember that you are walking with seeds, fruits and trees from the seed. Your future is then secured in the one who has deposited in you seeds. The source of my life's confidence is found in the fact that God finished my future already. I am not going to my future, but I am carrying the future with me. If I destroy my life with cocaine, alcohol or substances, then my future is cancelled. You should therefore never worry about the outcomes of your life. Why? You have fruits. For a seed to produce fruits, it must turn from a seed to plant. It may take some years to grow and produce the fruits. Do you see the point?

Chapter Seven

ENGAGE IN EFFECTIVE PLANNING AND ORGANISATION

"Planning is bringing the future into the present so that you can do something about it now."
~ Alan Lakein

The World of Dreamers and Losers

Our world is full of people whom I can refer to us dreamers. I can also call them losers. We have a lot of people who hope for things to change or even become better. They always spend time thinking; they never act and they never do anything about their future. They dream. They imagine a bright future without anything being done to create it. These people are amazing but not good to be with if you are serious about effectively living and life.

An effective life demands on the crafting of a roadmap, a plan to lead to a desired destination. I have had the privilege to travel with airplanes from one country to another, and I have been able to learn that each journey will be approved if the pilots have filled a flight plan. A flight plan shows how many passengers will be onboard the airplane. The airplane will also have food and logistics for passengers. It will also have details of the final destination. It will have all of the required resources and enough fuel. There will also be safety preparations such as life vests and information provided by the flight personnel. There will be instructions on what to do when the plane has a problem.

Further, to ensure the success of the airplane to arrive at the final destination, pilots will also keep communication with the control tower officials. From the onset of the journey, there is constant communication with the tower. A lot of work is put into preparation. I have a paradox question to ask: Why would all these preparations be undertaken? It is done not only to guarantee a successful flight to its destination, but also to prepare for a possible crisis. In this book, we are dealing with and discussing how to manage crisis such as these. Without planning, a crisis can destroy you, the organization or even a nation. Let me say it in another way: When there is a failure in planning, then there is a potential risk of failing. Alan Lakein says: "Failing to plan is planning to fail." If you even check any serious government or organization in the world, you will notice that they have a national development plan, business plan or a strategic plan. Why? Because of the desire to achieve success and progress.

What is Planning?

Millions of people on Earth never like to engage in the planning of their future. They leave planning to their governments and when there is a crisis, the government is blamed and criticized. There is a great danger when planning is left in the hands of government technocrats alone. There must be efforts to plan at individual, household, and community levels. Planning at the government level always occurs when nations or states budgets for given fiscal or financial years. The budget is usually read by the person in charge of planning. The titles of those responsible for presenting national budgets may vary from one country to another.

When we talk about planning, we are talking about the future, looking forward to what is to be accomplished and to what goals are to be attained. Planning is a critical activity that must be undertaken continually. Planning is the creation of long-range goals, objectives and activities for a period and estimation of how resources will be used especially funds, human resources and time. Planning produces a work plan that is a blueprint of activities to achieve defined objectives, targets and desired outcomes. Planning is a road map that results in achievement of purpose and vision. Planning should always start with an end in mind. The end in mind is known as a vision. That means planning should connect with a vision. A vision is about the preferred future that you hope to see or come to view.

The Book of Joel says, this words; *"And it shall come to pass afterward That I will pour out My Spirit on all flesh; Your sons and your daughters shall prophesy, your old men shall dream dreams, your young men shall see visions."* (Joel 2:28). The planning process requires understanding of personal and corporate vision. You need to have a clear vision of the future, which is always hoped to be better than the present state of affairs or things.

The process of planning involves thinking and organizing all activities that are necessary for achieving desired goals and results using available resources. Planning is a conceptual activity that requires conceptual skills. Planning is needed in business, organizations, families, communities, churches and nations. In other words, planning is needed in every area of life. You need spiritual, social, physical, health or financial planning and plans for success.

To overcome crisis, you will need to possess the planning capabilities. Planning, as mentioned above, results into the creation of a work plan. A work plan is simply an annual or multiyear summary of all tasks to be accomplished within a given time frame and defined responsibilities. A work plan can also be for a short period (e.g., maybe a quarter or half-year). Work plans contain an integrated list of activities. When implemented, a work plan will help you achieve desired goals and move you toward your preferred future. A planner must also have the ability to forecast. Forecasting is about predicting the future.

Contingency or Emergency Planning

We have spoken generally about planning in this chapter. I want to extrapolate the discussion to include contingency planning. Sometimes it is also referred to as emergency planning. Contingency planning is the development of plans of outcomes, events or crises that is usually unexpected or just foreseen or forecasted. The purpose of contingency plans is to manage potential risks that have catastrophic consequences. Contingency plans can be prepared for organizations, companies, businesses, communities or governments. For instance, suppose an organization loses its employees through a bombing by a terrorist group. How can the company or organization deal with such a situation? The organization will not be able to meet the needs of its customers or stakeholders. In order to prevent such events or happenings, individuals or organizations need to engage in contingency planning. The plan could require employees to be placed in different buildings to avoid all of them being destroyed in one building.

Get Involved in Preparedness Actions

Preparedness is part of planning. It is a critical step and process required in disaster, crisis or emergency management. One part of guaranteeing success is preparedness. Preparedness may mean several things. Generally, before a crisis hits, preparedness is taking actions so you are ready to respond to a crisis. It is not a one-time activity, but rather a continuous process. Preparedness are the actions that you take so that you are ready to respond to a crisis. Preparedness is not a one-time activity but rather it is a continuous process.

What is Preparedness?

- It involves learning about potential crisis types.
- It involves practicing and testing some actions before a disaster occurs.
- It involves acquiring knowledge of potential threats, risks and early warning signs.
- It requires carrying out risk and disaster analyses.
- It involves developing a contingency response plan.
- It includes having the knowledge and capacities developed.

Is Planning as Complicated as it Sounds?

Many people think that planning is a complicated process. They think it is not something they can do. Generally, intelligent individuals are given the responsibility to plan. But planning is really very simple. Let me share with you a story.

Suppose you have a trip that you want to undertake from one location to another. To be successful, you need to think a little. You will need to state clearly why you are undertaking the journey or trip. You should never do things without any aim. You need to ask the question: Why am I taking the trip? The answers to that question will help you know the objectives of the trip. You will be able to explain your purpose. You also need to ask: Where is the final destination? The answer will give you the details where you will end. The next thing you need to think about is strategies. How will you reach your destination? What means are you going to use? What time will you need to start the journey? What do you need to carry? When you answer all these questions, you will be able to determine how you will reach your destination.

What Is a Strategy?

A strategy refers to the actions you need to carry out in order to achieve the objectives. For instance, you might need to start the journey early to avoid the traffic jam; you might need a co-driver; you might need to get money from your bank a day before your planned trip. You might need to buy the air ticket early so that you save resources. These are all strategies. These are actions that you carry out to enable you achieve your objectives or goals. Strategy gives you the direction of what needs to be done in order to arrive at your final destination. The destination could even be your vision. A vision is a dream in pictures. A vision is a preferred future that is better than the current state of things. You can also learn how to come up with strategy by working with other people. You can ask how you can reach your destination faster. You will always find people who will give you their time, ideas and ways of approaching situations.

This brings us to the point that strategies help you to integrate all activities that you need to do in order to achieve the goals you have set. Strategy also allows you to take advantage of your strength and reduce the risks. Planning also involves listing all the tasks necessary to ensure that goals are achieved.

Now let us define planning. Planning is an effort undertaken to develop goals, strategies and all related activities that are required to achieve the objectives of an individual, business, organization or a nation. Planning is also the process of managing the distance between the present and the future desired destination. Additionally, planning is a process to ensure effective use of resources and employment of strategies to achieve desired goals and objectives to realize intended results.

Who Is Responsible for Planning?

We are living at a time when there is rapid change and tremendous competition in a complex and dynamic operational environment. This means things are changing very fast. The speed of life is faster than it was before. You have to be aware of the competitors, employees, customers, suppliers, or stakeholders. You have to be aware of what is happening in the market, environment or world around you.

It must be noted that the responsibility of planning is not in God; it is squarely in the hands of an individual, leaders or managers. Nobody should blame God that life is unfair. Effective planning will in most cases lead to a better quality of life. It will lead to improvements. It will create a desired future. Let me quote what King Solomon wrote about planning in Proverbs as follows:

We may make our plans, but God has the last word. You may think everything you do is right, but the Lord judges your motives. Ask the Lord to bless your plans, and you will be successful in carrying them out. Everything the Lord has made has its destiny; and the destiny of the wicked is destruction. The Lord hates everyone who is arrogant; he will never let them escape punishment. Be loyal and faithful, and God will forgive your sin. Obey the Lord and nothing evil will happen to you. When you please the Lord, you can make your enemies into friends. It is better to have a little, honestly earned, than to have a large income, dishonestly gained. You may make your plans, but God directs your actions. (Proverbs 16:1-9)

The Principles and Valuable Lessons

1. People are responsible for planning and plans. God is not responsible. God directs the plan and the actions. He leads you to your desire.
2. It is our personal responsibility to develop the plans, determine our goals, actions, strategies and resources to achieve our desired objectives.
3. Plans are established for the right motives and not destructive motives.
4. God blesses your plans so you can succeed by getting to your desires.
5. Your destiny depends on the plan that you have. Without a plan, you will never arrive at the desired destination.
6. Before the flight, every aircraft has a plan to get to the desired destination.
7. A plan implementation requires humility and not arrogance.
8. A plan requires loyalty and faithfulness. If you lack commitment and dedication, you will not achieve the objectives contained in the plan.
9. Plans will succeed when you please God. How do you please God? Be faithful. Trust God. Be obedient. Let your actions show your faith in the Lord.
10. Do not become dishonest to achieve the plans faster. Take your time with the resources that you get to achieve the plans.
11. God will also lead you and direct the actions you will carry out to achieve the plans. For instance, God might give you insights, wisdom, knowledge, good health, resources, opportunities, friends and many things that will help you achieve your objectives.

The Powerful Force of Planning

In my view, planning is probably the most powerful force on earth. Planning is powerful because God himself acknowledged that truth. Let us refresh our minds. What did God say about planning? Genesis 11:1-9 gives an account of the moral force of planning. A group of people came together with intentions of "building" the tower that could reach the sky. The group had leaders, one voice, one goal, one language and the desire to be famous. They wanted to make a name for themselves. The group built a tower because they had a goal to reach the sky. If you read the story carefully, you will realize that God also got concerned. Why? Yes, the people had a plan, but with bad motives.

What did God do? God had to leave the throne in order to go see the city and the tower that had been built. The Lord said if they can do all these and it is just the beginning, then they have the capability to do anything they want. God stopped the work, the project and caused confusion by mixing up the language of all the people that were engaged with the project.

Another story and examples comes from Jeremiah. Look at what God says:

This is God's Word on the subject: "As soon as Babylon's seventy years are up and not a day before, I'll show up and take care of you as I promised and bring you back home. I know what I'm doing. I have it all planned out—plans to take care of you, not abandon you, plans to give you the future you hope for. (Jeremiah 29:10-11)

Now let me give you what I believe is the powerful nature of planning:

1. Planning allows you to arrive at your destination and preferred future.
2. Planning enables strategy development that will help you to accomplish your goals.
3. Planning allows you to set clear goals.
4. Planning allows you to ensure effective use of your time and important resources.
5. Planning gives you an opportunity to discipline yourself. It means planning will allow you determine what you must do and what you must not do.
6. Planning gives you the ability to focus. Without focus, it is impossible to get ahead, accomplish the given tasks, or achieve planned goals.
7. Planning helps you to minimize the distractions that come with the challenges of living.
8. Planning helps you to come up with creative ways of solving problems.
9. Planning enables maximization of resources, effective and efficient ways of the use of those resources.
10. Planning makes you committed because you have it on paper.
11. Planning enables efficiency (for organizations, entities or individuals).
12. Planning allows standards to be maintained.
13. Planning ensures all activities conducted are relevant and related to achievement of desired goals.

14. Planning enables the creation of sustainability of results.
15. Planning supports organizational learning and development of capacity.
16. Planning helps to forecast and prepare for the future.
17. Planning unlocks keys to success. Without planning, failure is inevitable.

What Are the Basic Elements of the Plan?

A plan is prepared to achieve the purpose and vision of the organization or even an individual vision. A plan has the following:

1. Long-term objectives.
2. Short-term goals.
3. Strategy or strategies for achieving the purpose.
4. Activities to be carried out to achieve the goals or objectives.
5. Sources of resources.
6. Responsibility centers.

Chapter Eight

HOW TO GROW AND DEVELOP IN TIMES OF CRISIS

"The most difficult step ever is the first step. It comes with doubts, uncertainties, and all sort of fears. If you defy all odds and take it, your confidence will replicate very fast and you'll become a master!"
~ Martin Luther King Jr

How Do You Do It?

We have been exploring several concepts in this book. We have arrived at a critical point. The question before you is this: How can you grow and develop during a crisis? How do you achieve growth and development? You might have doubts about the concept and possibility of growth in crisis. But I have good news. It is possible! How? The chapter here will reveal to you the methods and strategies that are available for growth and development in critical times of crisis.

1. Result-oriented Management

You probably have heard about management possibly from college or elsewhere. The secret strategy for growth and development is management. You will need to manage yourself in order to emerge from the crisis. That means you need to be an effective manager. This kind of managers are rare. They have unique abilities- good planning and organization, communication, teamwork, budget and time management. Are you an effective manager? In what ways can you improve as a manager?

The power of management is a top and hidden secret that is needed for you to grow and develop. Management is critical in every area of life. Organizations, companies or nations all require good managers. Managers create order and organization. Management for results is vital for change and improvement. Result-oriented management is simply the management where focus is on results and outcomes. It requires the management with the focus on discipline to achieve agreed goals to generate desired results.

In times of crisis, you need to study and learn how to manage time, resources, relationships, opportunities, events, problems or situations. You need to learn to manage people and everything around you. Management is important because without management you will incur additional and unnecessary costs and losses.

For example, if you mismanage your vehicle or money you will lose either. If you misuse your body with cocaine, alcohol or drugs, you will be impacted negatively. If you manage your life effectively as possible, you will have a positive impact. Also, during crisis, you need to manage everything around you. You need to be an effective manager.

During a crisis, people watch how you either effectively or ineffectively manage a crisis in order to come out as a victor or a victim. Failure to effectively manage a crisis is a result of poor management competence. We have thousands of people with limited and incompetent management capacity. On the other hand, they are people who become heroes during the critical moments of a crisis. These people have skills, capacity, competence and abilities in management. They are people who prepare ahead of crises.

You might be wondering why I am talking about effective management as a way to grow in crises. You could use a crisis to develop your character. You could use a crisis to read a book or study. For example, some leaders were thrown in jail, but they used their time effectively to grow and develop. The story of Robert Mugabe, the longest serving President of Zimbabwe, comes to mind here Mugabe was jailed but he used the crisis to develop himself. There are several other examples that you can find about people who were able to grow during a crisis.

My conclusion is this: If you have ears, you need to hear or eyes you need to see (Matthew 7: 13-14). Good management will produce good results and benefits even during a crisis. If you are not a good manager, you will be a victim not a victor during crisis.

Theologically, if you mismanage something, God takes it away from the steward. That is how simple or serious this can be. If you also mismanage your health by eating for examples, you will end up with diseases that can destroy you. I hope this sheds some light on the importance of management.

2. Potential Exploitation

In every seed, there is a tree. This is a mystery. Then God said, *"Let the earth bring forth grass, the herb yielding seed, and the fruit tree yielding fruit after his kind, whose seed is in itself, upon the earth: and it was so."* (Genesis 1:11). See the state of a seed in itself. This statement contains deep insights about potential. Every human is created with potential. What is potential? Potential is what you have not done but you are capable of doing. Potential is not what you have achieved but what you are capable of achieving. Potential means capability and ability.

During a crisis, everybody has potential or the ability that needs exploitation. A lot of people give up or surrender to the situation. They became victims that changed my life is understanding that I have great potential. I have hidden or dormant power. Everybody is created with potential just like me and just like a seed. Most people never have an understanding of their hidden potential or ability. God created everything with potential. That is why God also told the first humans to be fruitful, which means you are full of fruits. Maximization and exploitation of the potential is critical for crisis management. This will help you be a victor.

3. Become Responsible in Life

Another way to grow is to become responsible. Many people are just irresponsible. They are not mature. They are immature in all areas of their lives. They are not trustworthy. They lack integrity. They compromise on critical matters and principles. In times of crisis, growth and development tend to occur only if there is a sense of responsibility. There is also irresponsible behavior. Some engage in prostitution, idleness, alcohol consumption and other vices. Irresponsible people also transfer responsibility, keep blaming others for their situation, and act like victims.

Crisis demands individuals with a sense of responsibility and better understanding of their seasons and purpose. Leaders need to be responsible as they lead during crises. Everything on earth and its abundant resources belong to God but man is responsible for what happens. God gave humans the responsibility to manage the earth and resources. Therefore, it requires responsibility and management. To be responsible is not simple. It demands work. Work involves a lot of laboring, sweating and cultivating in order to manage effectively. From this time forward, each must take on responsibility and be good managers. Without laboring and toiling, you will not be able to reap the fruits needed for sustaining the life, growth and development. Without responsibility, there cannot be effective management. Growth is possible with better management. Harvesting of more fruits requires effective management.

From a Biblical perspective, God will allow growth if there is effective management. Growth can be prevented if there is mismanagement. God did not permit the rain to come in the

Garden because there was no manager to take charge and own responsibility. If you want God to increase your resources, you need to be faithful and have faith in God. God only trusts people who have good management capability. Therefore, it is up to man either to be responsible or irresponsible. God gave man the most powerful power, which I refer to as will and choice. Every human has power to choose or make choices based on the will in which they have been endowed. A will is available to activate the choices of mankind.

4. Accept that Change Is Inevitable

Change is something that is unavoidable and inevitable. In crisis times, there will be a need for everything effective management that I have mentioned earlier in this book. However, how would you accept that fact that crisis is inevitable? You must have an awareness of the various ways that will facilitate you to manage it.

The following list might be useful during crises:

1. Decide and determine on the most critical needs, which are different from wants.
2. Obtain only what is required out of the list of all your needs.
3. Decide to live within your means.
4. Withdraw and stop using your resources from things that are unnecessary.
5. Postpone some of the major investments or project you are undertaking.
6. Attach value to what you possess or own.
7. Develop a saving culture.
8. Guard and conserve your assets and resources.
9. Establish priorities.

Revise these ideas constantly for effective management of crisis. Why? Humans have a tendency to forget what to do during a crisis. It is important to keep the list as a weapon ready for use when a crisis strikes. It also requires that other concepts are combined (e.g. integration, adding value, hard work and exploitation of potential).

5. Secret Riches Available in Secret Places

Isaiah 45:3 says, *"And I will give thee the treasures of darkness, and hidden riches of secret places, that thou mayest know that I, the Lord, which call thee by thy name, am the God of Israel."* God has stored treasures and riches in secret places. God has promised to give those treasures and hidden riches to us, but this requires calling on Him. Everything that is required to solve human problems has been hidden. There is a solution to every problem. There is a way that leads somewhere, but there must be a will. There is an old saying, *"Where there is a will, there is a way."* You might be going through a crisis, but let me remind you that God has hidden riches and treasures reserved and kept. You cannot get the riches by not seeking God. You have to search until you find God.

God does not bless people who are poor at management of entrusted resources. Instead, God will banish them and give their resources to another responsible person. Do you remember the reason that man was banished from the Garden of Eden in Genesis 3? God posted Cherubim to guard after Adam was driven away. Adam was irresponsible and blamed the spouse. A good manager does not blame others for their shortcomings but takes and owns up to the responsibility. There are some things God gave you or humanity from the secret places that you are not taking care of. Believe me, God will take them away and you will be affected by a crisis.

Further, critically you need to take a look at your personal life. Proverbs 30:25 says, *"The ants are a people not strong, yet they prepare their meat in the summer."* The ants have a saving culture in the summer with an awareness that winter will come and food will be unavailable. The ants store food in preparation for the challenging seasons. What have you saved out of the resources that you have acquired? Are you like an ant or not? Only a fool does not behave like an ant. Effective leaders set aside resources for unexpected events.

Furthermore, Proverbs 17:16 says, *"Why should fools have money in hand to buy wisdom, when they are not able to understand it?"* There are humans who are just foolish; they cannot use the resources they possess to buy wisdom. They do things that sometimes never make sense. Wisdom is powerful in times of crisis.

6. Stop Pretending

Author of Proverbs, King Solomon says, the following words *"One person pretends to be rich, yet has nothing; another pretends to be poor, yet has great wealth"* (Proverbs 13:7). A lot of people also make a terrible mistake. They pretend and they never really know who they are. Who are you? If you do not know who you are, you will be destroyed by a crisis. Further, some people have been bribed. They took money and opportunities in a dishonest way. Let me say something. That money will go away. King Solomon warns us: *"Dishonest money dwindles away, but whoever gathers money little by little makes it grow"* (Proverbs 13:11). When a crisis hits, people who obtained wealth and resources quickly and dishonestly will be the first victims. Why? They have no character, tests, tribulations and experiences including lessons to draw from or gain knowledge. Knowledge is also important during times of crisis and non-crisis times. When you take time and follow through the process, you get the character and maturity needed to overcome a crisis.

When you gather money little by little, you please God. However, if you get it quickly through dubious means, you displease God. There are people in important roles who lack integrity and character. I will be writing extensively about this in my next book, Building Leadership Character. In times of crisis, people who are dishonest will be exposed and destroyed. Dishonesty is the absence of character. Do not engage in dishonest behavior during crises. Keep your integrity. Stay honest at the times of crisis. A crisis will end, but your integrity does not have to. Never engage in acts that are dishonest. For example, you might engage in prostitution during times of crisis, then after the crisis in two or three years, you find you have to live on HIV/AIDs drugs for 20 or 30 years. Which one is better? You might engage in criminality and die. It is better to be faithful and honest even in times of disaster and crisis.

Poverty is not a Permanent Condition

A lot of people think that poverty is a permanent event. It is not. It is temporary.

The LORD God made all kinds of trees grow out of the ground— trees that were pleasing to the eye and good for food. In the middle of the garden were the tree of life and the tree of the knowledge of good and evil. A river watering the garden flowed from Eden; from there it was separated into four headwaters. The name of the first is the Pishon; it winds through the entire land of Havilah, where there is gold. The gold of that land is good; aromatic resin and onyx are also there. The name of the second river is the Gihon; it winds through the entire land of Cush. The name of the third river is the Tigris; it runs along the east side of Ashur. And the fourth river is the Euphrates. (Genesis 2:9-12)

God has given you resources that are available in the land around you. You might have not been using the resources properly. You need to check the environment. To come out poverty, you need to have a better understanding of God's fundamental truth about wealth.

In the scripture above, God gave wealth: foods and fruits, water, gold and other precious metals, resins, oils, onyxes and other precious stones. The causes of crises are many. Some nations or people have messed up God-given resources for survival. Some communities have destroyed the water bodies, rivers, lakes and swamps. Some people have used chemicals on water and also caused land fragmentation, degradation and poor exploitation of resources. Wars have emerged as there are fights over oil.

What are we talking about here? We are talking about greedy human behavior. Greed in your community or country might be the cause of an economic, social or political crisis happening today in most parts of the world. You might find that leaders have amassed wealth at the expense of the masses. You now find few wealthy people while others are wallowing in poverty.

Chapter Nine

PREPARATION FOR DEPLOYMENT AND FREEDOM

"When you come out of the storm,
you won't be the same person who walked in.
That's what this storm's all about."
~ Haruki Murakami, Kafka on the Shore

What is Wrong with World Education Systems?

The world system(s) of education in many countries has prepared graduates for employment as opposed to the choosing our destinies to create our own jobs and deploy ourselves. As a young man, I was advised to work hard in school and get a job. That is exactly what I did. I excelled at college. The same advice is what I gave to my younger siblings and our children, too. What has been the main objective? It has been to obtain a job or employment opportunity for a salary. Besides that, the goal has been to develop a successful career and live happily. The career that I chose has taken me to different countries. As I grow older, I begin to realize that I cannot be employed forever. I have found I have to study life and watch life. I have become a student of life. I have travelled a long distance to study life from the "University of Life."

What is the best alternative to employment? Through interaction with various people and leaders, I have observed that self-employed entrepreneurs are the ones who are truly deployed and make progress. Whenever a person is hired for a job, he or she is employed. He becomes an employee of the public or private company. He or she is a public servant or private employee. How many people have been employed in your community? How many people have been employed in government or public service? How many have been employed in NGOs, CBOs or CSOs? I too have been employed. I noted that when you are employed, your paycheck comes from the employer. The employer might be a large or small corporation or organization. When you are employed, you will always be told what to do and when to do it. You will be given a job description or terms of reference. Terms of reference means when you forget what you are supposed to do, you refer to the terms of service. There are restrictions that you will be required to observe. You scale of influence remains also limited.

What if you are deployed? What if you are using your gifts, talents or ideas to make a difference? You will realize that your circle of influence is wider. You will never receive a job description. You will have a large group of people to influence or reach. You will also be serving people as well as working with them. When you are deployed or there is deployment, it means you serve people with your gifts. People are attracted to the gift that nobody can take away. It will be you only to abuse or become proud or arrogant with it. If you are consistent and rooted in God's word, you become like a branch of a vine tree that Jesus spoke of in the following words:

I am the true vine, and my Father is the gardener. He cuts off every branch in me that bears no fruit, while every branch that does bear fruit he prunes so that it will be even more fruitful. You are already clean because of the word I have spoken to you. Remain in me, as I also remain in you. No branch can bear fruit by itself; it must remain in the vine. Neither can you bear fruit unless you remain in me. "I am the vine; you are the branches. If you remain in me and I in you, you will bear much fruit; apart from me you can do nothing. If you do not remain in me, you are like a branch that is thrown away and withers; such branches are picked up, thrown into the fire and burned. If you remain in me and my words remain in you, ask whatever you wish, and it will be done for you. This is to my Father's glory, that you bear much fruit, showing yourselves to be my disciples. (John 15:1-8)

God is the gardener and wants people who have the capacity to bear much fruits. How do you bear much fruits? You have to be attached to the vine tree. You have to be a branch. You have to be close to the vine. If you got cut off as a branch, you will never bear fruits. A tree does not grow over night. It takes time for it to produce branches and fruits. These is what establishes the principle of potential. You need time to grow into a branch. You will never be a vine tree. What do learn from here? You need to branch off from what God has called you. However, you must be ready and mature. Even when you branch off, you must keep attached to the mother tree. The mother tree can be like a coach, mentor or parent. I have seen people who decided that they never want to be connected to the mentors and they have ended up becoming a disaster to the world.

For you to be ready for deployment, it requires some experience, training, coaching, learning and preparation. It also requires the use of your gifts, talents and resources. What talents are you not using? What gifts are you not exploiting and using? That is the source of your deployment. When I think of deployment, I believe God is the "Deployer" for completion of His will. You will recall Apostle Paul whom God deployed as a preacher. Look at Peter, the leader of the early Church of Jesus Christ. There are many examples of people whom God deployed.

Service Is the Key to Deployment

There are millions of people who want to be great in our world. They want to be famous. They want to be popular. But they are not willing to be servants. They never want to fold their sleeves to do dirty works or clean up their cities or municipalities. The Lord Jesus Christ told His leadership students (i.e., disciples) that, "whoever wants to be the greatest must be a servant..." (Matthew 20:20-28). The details are given in the scripture text below:

Then the mother of Zebedee's sons came to Jesus with her sons and, kneeling down, asked a favor of him. "What is it you want?" he asked. She said, "Grant that one of these two sons of mine may sit at your right and the other at your left in your kingdom." "You don't know what you are asking," Jesus said to them. "Can you drink the cup I am going to drink?" "We can," they answered. Jesus said to them, "You will indeed drink from my cup, but to sit at my right or left is not for me to grant. These places belong to those for whom they have been prepared by my Father." When the ten heard about this, they were indignant with the two brothers. Jesus called them together and said, "You know that the rulers of the Gentiles lord it over them, and their high officials exercise authority over them. Not so with you. Instead, whoever wants to become great among you must be your servant, and whoever wants to be first must be your slave— just as the Son of Man did not come to be served, but to serve, and to give his life as a ransom for many. (Matthew 20:20-28)

The story above is similar to what happens in our world today. You will find parents asking for opportunities for their children. Look at the mother of John and James. She went and approached Him, asking for the sons to take positions by sitting at the right and left of Jesus. She wanted them to occupy the top positions. I would consider the two positions as vice president and prime minister. What positions would you think she was asking?

Jesus continued to advice His students that to become great, they need to become servants. You need to be the first to serve and be a "slave". This is where there has been confusion. A lot of us hate to be slaves. For third world countries, they have a challenge where millions have been colonized and suffered the impact of slavery. I do agree with you that slavery is bad. However, what

Jesus is referring to here is that you become a slave of your gift. That is, you must be willing to serve your gift and people will be looking to get the services from you. Serving your gift makes you a slave. It requires commitment, dedication, development, and discipline. Even if you have great gifts endowed with you, but without commitment and character to serve, you will not become great in your area.

Yet Jesus said whoever wants to become great must become the servant. Jesus even showed the same teaching to the disciples. He said He came to serve not to be served. Are you willing to serve? If you are first to serve, people will always be looking for you when they have needs to meet or problems to solve. A person who becomes great is the one with a different attitude. He or she is always willing to serve. They never complain. They never grumble. If you are always complaining or grumbling, nobody will ever trust you with responsibility or think of you when there is an opportunity. Do you see my point? What are your habits? What is your level of commitment to work or service?

Simon is my brother-in-law who is married to my younger sister, Elizabeth. This guy is a wonderful brother. You will never find him murmuring or complaining. He has a different attitude. He is always being called to serve and solve problems. Why? He is dependable. He is available. He is always willing to serve and help. As a result, he has become an influence in our projects and community activities. I have entrusted him with lots of responsibilities and resources. Now some people see him and they start to hate him. Yet those people also had the opportunity to do what this guy does. However, they lacked commitment and a servant attitude.

Utilize Your Gift to Open Doors

Every human being is like a seed. They have fruits. They are also created with gifts. Nobody is created without gifts. Have you ever imagined why athletes, after international competitions such as the Olympics, are welcomed to the State House for dinner with the Head of State? I have seen these happen in Uganda, Kenya and other countries. Athletes have gifts that they serve and ushers them to great people. The president of a nation is a great person. How can local people have access to the president, yet many highly intelligent people have no access to him? The answer is utilizing your gift to opens doors. King Solomon said, *"A gift opens the way and ushers the giver into the presence of the great"* (Proverbs 18:16). Can you see what this statement says? It says a person with a gift will have a way opened for him or her and that gifts will bring them to great people, great leaders and people of influence and impact.

What is your gift? Your gift cannot be taken from you. Your gift can remain dormant, but it will still be there. You gift is like a dormant seed which has not been put in the soil to germinate. The only problem is that most of the people on earth have not gotten the opportunity to develop their gifts. You need to discover your gift, practice and develop it.

For instance, if your gift is football, you need to spend hours practicing to serve your gift. It can someday bring you before great people. If your gift is singing, it can one day bring you in front of great leaders. I know my gift and I keep working on it. I see myself in front of great leaders. I have already been able to meet some people who I count as great and I still hope to meet more in my life. The problem with some of humanity is the lack of effort to develop their individual gifts.

One of the statements that I use to encourage myself is this: *"I must be willing to do things today that others are not willing to do in order to have things others will not have tomorrow."* Are you willing to pay the price? Are you willing to sacrifice pleasure for the sake of purpose? Are you willing to be disciplined? Are you willing to be corrected?

In Chapter 12, I wrote about how to discover your gift. You need to study that chapter. You need to spend time reflecting on your gift. I explain what you need to do. One of the things about gift development is that it does not come easy. You will need to work hard, sometimes even work harder. When you work hard, you will get a reward. If you are serving and doing God's purpose, you will even get an eternal reward. You will also need to serve with humility the gifts that God has given you. Your gifts are meant to help people. Your gifts could be to solve problems. With your gifts at hand, you will always overcome any kind of crises that you encounter. The earth or nations in the world will encounter various kinds of crises. Only the Kingdom of God as a country is never in crisis. A crisis cannot happen in God's Kingdom. Everywhere else will experience a crisis.

Work Hard

As a citizen of any nation, you will be required to produce something. The wealth of a nation is measured by what is known as Gross Domestic Product (GDP). This is the sum total of all products produce by the citizens of a given country. What are you producing? What is your contribution? Or are you waiting for someone to produce and you just enjoy? You must always do something if you are going to avoid a crisis. When God created Adam and Eve in the garden of Eden, He created them to cultivate the garden. He created them to weed it. The details of God's instructions are in Genesis 2 and 3. If God could ask man to work, what about you? What are you doing? Are you working? The deployment process is enhanced through hard work.

What happens to you or organization as you work or cultivate? You will become fruitful. You will also become productive. When you are fruitful, people will come looking for the fruit and they will pay you for possessing the fruit. When you are productive, you will have products that will be needed in the market. What are you producing? You will only be fulfilled and happy when you are fruitful and productive. One of the most important things in the world is productivity. Every nation struggles to produce something. That is why Japan produces cars that are exported to other countries. That is why Apple Corporation produces its Apple products. Even China, Cuba or Chad are struggling to produce something. When you work for God, complete His assignment and you are recalled, you will hear statements like this: "Well-done faithful servant." God does not want people who starts things; He is interested in people who finish things.

Further, through your hard work you will find that your potential gets released. You will become a different person or organization. You will become fulfilled and a person that God intended you to be when He created you. When you are deploying your gifts, you will always be self-motivated. You will need no one to remind you to implement your tasks. You will have eternal energy. However, for a job or employment sometimes you will be forced to go and work. With your gift, it will be difficult to lay it down.

Sometimes, I wonder why young people and other older adults dislike to work. People avoid work. They expect everything to be given free. Our world is twisted. People have failed to know what is valuable. Have you asked yourself what is valuable? I believe work is critical. I believe prayer is important. Life is valuable. Values are critical.

Let me go back to the issue of work. Work is important because God Himself created the universe and all the beauty that is visible and invisible. The Bible says God worked for six days and rested on the seventh day. God released His potential. He performed great works and produced wonders. The power of work is therefore vital for anyone who desires to achieve greatness and overcome crisis. The instruction to man to be fruitful meant that man possesses seeds. Hence, the gifts are more like seeds. If you plant and protect the seeds from weeds, you will obtain fruits in the end and you will be able to fulfill your assignment (or your divine purpose) on Earth. When a seed is planted in the soil, it pushes out of the ground through various conditions until it gets out, producing a tree or plant. Your life is like that. You must go through a process, buried until you manifest fruits. Remember it is a process. Nothing happens in an instant.

Development of a Positive Attitude

The world we live in today is full of problems. There are many challenges or issues that affect the world. There are problems of food, water, sanitation, hygiene, security, and safety. Everywhere you go in any community, there will be problems and as problems are solved, new problems will emerge. Problems or difficulties are good. They cause people to grow. You will never grow in good times. You will grow when there is pressure. The pressures or challenges in the world requires leaders to emerge. They require innovation or people with new ideas and solutions.

In essence, our world is crying for solutions to our problems. If you have gifts, then you can be able to solve some of the problems in your local community. I believe every human being created by God has a responsibility. They are created to solve a certain problem. They are not here only to enjoy the things of the world, but also to solve the problems of the world.

There are so many needs among people. People have desires. Every generation that God creates is expected to leave something good or better for the next generation. That is why God gives vision to leaders to improve the present so that the future will be better. Your knowledge and experiences are more important to help you move to the future. You also need to know that what is around you is not as important as what is in you. You will have low and high moments. You will have the vicissitudes of life. You will have crisis and non-crisis moments. As I said, what is around you is not as important as what is inside you. Paul said it differently when he said "greater is He that is in you than He who is in the world." You must believe that.

171

In the midst of this challenging period of your life, I believe you should have a different attitude. What is that attitude?

1. Your future is in you and you are carrying your future with you.
2. You are a walking destiny.
3. Your future is more important than your past.
4. Your future is more valuable than your past.
5. What is around you is not important as what is within you or inside you.
6. What is inside you is more important than what is outside or in the world.
7. God chooses your destiny and how it is fulfilled is your responsibility. It is up to you.
8. Your past is dead and Jesus died to salvage your future.
9. Deal with your past so that you are able to go to your future.
10. Dealing with the past helps you to go to the future.
11. Every person has a history. Deal with your past publically.

Sow Your Seeds in the Morning and Evening

How can you sow seeds in the morning and in the evening? We need to learn a lesson from this statement made by David's son. Solomon said those words in Ecclesiastes 11:6, *"Sow your seeds in the morning and at evening let not your hands be idle, for you do not know which will succeed, weather this or that or weather both will do equally well."* How many of us sow seeds in the morning but also do the same in the evening? Only a few human beings. Practice this in your life. You will see the impact. A crisis cannot destroy you using this strategy. This strategy has helped me over the years. The above verse is an important one to me especially as I carry out contingency planning and preparedness of my future. I not only prepare things in the day, but I also work at night. I am never idle during the night just as I work during the day. I keep working. This book, for example, was written after official working hours.

Doing God's Work Is No Protection Against the Pain of Crisis

There are people who are walking around in the world claiming they are God's favorite. They claim God's blessings. They claim His promises. The claim His healing power. They claim that God will supply all their needs and many more. I want to sound a message and a warning. God will not protect you; sometimes He can press you through a crisis. He can allow you to face the crisis. God does this in order to test your strength. How strong are you? Are you really strong? How many tests can you handle in a month or a year? Have you come out of crisis? If you have not come out of one, then you should expect a crisis. Are you ready? Apostle Paul said the following words:

We are hard pressed on every side, but not crushed; perplexed, but not in despair; persecuted, but not abandoned; struck down, but not destroyed. We always carry around in our body the death of Jesus, so that the life of Jesus may also be revealed in our body. For we who are alive are always being given over to death for Jesus' sake, so that his life may also be revealed in our mortal body. So then, death is at work in us, but life is at work in you. (2 Corinthians 4:8-12)

Can you think of the circumstance that made Paul to write such words or statements? Paul as a leader of the early church suffered much pain and crisis. He said they were hard pressed from all sides. You can say all angles. They were persecuted, or beaten, punished, humiliated or badly treated. Every day they faced death. Every day they saw disaster. What kept them going? It was their faith and perseverance.

What I have learned over the years as a human being is that crisis is a must in every person's life. As we achieve our dreams, aspirations and plans and even trust God for many blessings, there will be moments and times in which a crisis will strike us unexpected. Sometimes, it will not have anything to do with what you have or have not done. It may be that God wants to measure your level of confidence and maturity. Even if we are so hardworking, there will be turns and events that come to your life, family, friends or organizations unexpected. You might be working for government or private sector, then everything turns upside down and you experience the hardest moments. How do you maintain your balance? How do maintain your success? You must develop some capacities.

If you have not developed the capacities required to thrive, you will be destroyed. Success in those moments or times of crisis is determined by your ability to manage turmoil and keep your balance. Your maturity level will also be tested. When things fall apart, when people lose jobs and when there is chaos and confusion.

How do you know the mature individuals or leaders? I believe you will know them by the response and reaction. Those who mature never panic but they plan. They never react to crises but instead respond to them as an opportunity. They never get carried away. They never blame anyone. They never take responsibility and ownership. To me maturity is the capacity to manage not only the unexpected, but also the expected. Those who are mature also have faith and confidence in their abilities to manage chaos, confusion, tragedy and crisis. Instead, they keep going despite the crisis. They carry out their plans. That is called leadership.

Through my own reflections and search on knowledge, I have thought about true leadership for so many years. I studied for over 10 years to understand true leadership. Various scholars have provided many definitions of leadership. Scholars have their own ways of presenting issues. To me to understand leadership, it is to understand the nature of leadership. The nature of something is related to the qualities of what is being studied.

What is True Leadership?

- Leadership is the capacity of an individual to influence a group of people to follow you through the inspiration of God's vision for the community.
- Leadership is the capacity to free up or set people free from oppression, slavery and injustice by enabling them discover themselves and enable them take charge of their destiny and responsibilities.
- Leadership is enabling people to overcome crisis and enjoy the benefits of crisis and other opportunities. Leadership helps people maximize their potential and achieve their personal and corporate visions.
- Leadership is changing the conditions, circumstances and lives of followers from worse to better.

Live by Faith and Not by Sight

True leaders live by faith and not by sight. What you see depresses you. When you live by faith, there is no fear and depression. Apostle Paul wrote to the Romans a message, which leaders must embrace. Here it is:

For therein is the righteousness of God revealed from faith to faith: as it is written, the just shall live by faith. For the wrath of God is revealed from heaven against all ungodliness and unrighteousness of men, who hold the truth in unrighteousness; Because that which may be known of God is manifest in them; for God hath shewed it unto them. For the invisible things of him from the creation of the world are clearly seen, being understood by the things that are made, even his eternal power and Godhead; so that they are without excuse. (Romans 1: 17-20)

It is impossible to lead followers when the leader is fearful. Followers are attracted to leaders who have no fear. They are attracted to leaders with great courage and faith. Faith comes from beliefs.

Over the years, I have arrived at a conclusion that when there is a crisis or unexpected events that threaten mankind, you will see its impact on their beliefs. Crisis shakes up the foundation of people's core beliefs. It causes people to doubt and fear. I recall years back in 2008 when I was facing a crisis of losing my job. I had left a job with a low pay and taken up another with a higher pay. This is a natural experience and response to life. All of us want to grow or do great things. Do not tell me you do not want that. If you say you do not, then you are a liar and you are dishonest. How will do this or that? You begin to doubt God. You doubt yourself. You have been going to church every Sunday but now you have doubt in God. You start to worry. This happens to all people. Even billionaires worry and get afraid in times of crisis. For instance, may be their businesses are up for foreclosure or they evaded taxes or embezzled company funds.

What Paul is teaching us in the above message is instructive. He says that our homes are like earthly tents in that they are easily destroyed. His real confidence is in the home built by God. Can you destroy the works of God? Can you change the works of God? You might kill people; that is easy. What about removing all the water from the oceans? What about bringing down the sun and moon to your house? Those things obviously are impossible!

Paul says we are confident and to know that we are with Lord. He says that we live by faith. My admonition to you is that you should not live by sight. Living by sight is dangerous. It is tough. It makes life look horrible. It brings hopelessness to people. You do not always see what is possible or how things could potentially be. You must have a different attitude. The attitude should be positive. For example, try an attitude like this: *"It does not matter; my future will be better than the present. I will win no matter what is around me."*

You will win if you do not give up or surrender to the situation. If you will be able to overcome any crisis that hits you, you must live by faith. It is the faith that gives you legal rights to receive even blessings from God. When you please God by believing in Him, then a reward awaits you (Hebrew 11:6).

We have explored several ideas and concepts in this chapter. The conclusions and next actions are largely up to you. I will recommend some things that I personally believe are critical and might be useful for you. They have worked for me and maybe they will work for you, too. If you have not planned your life or have not taken actions to insulate yourself from crises, here are some actions you can consider:

1. Ask God to forgive you for depending on a job instead of pursuing your purpose through effective planning, persistence and perseverance.

2. Develop plans to protect yourself, family or organizations from crisis.

3. Do not allow crises to change you, let your choices and decisions change you for the better.

4. Start to build your faith to handle faithless   moments of crisis through studying God's words and positive thinking.

5. Start planting seeds even as tiny as mustard seeds; they will grow and become the largest in the garden with big branches (Mark 4: 30-32).

6. Develop the habit of living by faith and not by sight.

Chapter Ten

HOW TO PROFIT AND TAKE ADVANTAGE OF CRISIS

Understanding the Benefits of Crisis

Throughout human history, the response to a crisis has been that it is a bad occurrence. Many people in the world believe that adversity is a bad thing. Adversity is another word that is used to refer to crisis. When adversity hits us, it can lead to either destruction or construction. I use these words very carefully. Adversity often leads to severe losses. It can also result into maximum gain. The war crisis in countries such as Somalia, South Sudan, Iraq, Syria and other countries have destroyed those nations profoundly as well as affected them negatively.

However, the crises in those countries has created opportunities for some people. During a crisis, there is danger, but there is also opportunity. From the above quote, the former President of United States Richard Nixon said, "Life is one crisis after another." To me this just sums up everything about crisis. If you are living on planet, you must therefore prepare yourself to face one crisis after the other. The only people who have no crises are those in resting in peace in the cemetery.

A time of crisis is a great opportunity where true leaders emerge. A crisis will force people to think. If you have been having a quality time in your job but when the message of downsizing is announced that you will not have a job within a six-month period, you will not sleep all night as you used to. Instead, you will begin to think at night. If you take the crisis as a positive occurrence, you will begin to develop a new approach to life and how you will cope without a job. In other words, a crisis will cause you to think, and through the process of thinking, you will generate new ideas, imaginations and review your life's pattern.

A major benefit of crisis that results from positive thinking are generation of ideas, innovation and creativity. Adversity will force leaders to rethink and generate new strategies and plans. It will push leaders and individuals to explore solutions to impacts of crisis. A crisis will force leaders to come with creative solutions to problems faced and minimize the impacts of crisis that often destroys people. It is during time of crisis that humans even remember to pray to God. Faith is exercised during the times of adversity. I recall as a child during the war in Teso Sub Region in the late 1990s, a majority of people would go to church for prayers every Sunday. However, when the crisis ended, the only a few people continued with a habit of prayer. A crisis forces people to change their habits and approach to life.

Chinese Ideology of Crises

Chinese people come from China. If you have limited knowledge about China, let me give you a background information: concerning population, China is the largest country in the world followed by India. It has a population of 1.374 billion as of 2015 estimated figures (China Population, Trading Economics). Can you imagine the people that live in China? They are over a billion people. In Uganda, where I was born, our population is about 40 million people. President J.F Kennedy said, "The Chinese use two brush stokes to write the word 'crisis.' One brush stroke stands for danger, the other for opportunity. In a crisis, be aware of danger - but recognize the opportunity." As you go through any crisis, think like the Chinese people. Never think of only danger, but think about the opportunities that lie untapped.

God created you with unlimited potential. In times of crisis, your potential will come handy for exploiting of opportunities. If you want to benefit during times of adversity, make careful decisions and choices. In addition, think about opportunities that you will gain from those hard times. A crisis is also an opportunity to take risks. Those risks are hidden with golden opportunities.

Resilience in Crisis

Human beings are created with potential. The potential is often hidden or untapped. When there is a crisis, the potential can be cultivated and applied. It will force people to become resilient. Nothing makes people resilient than adversity. Why? There is a survival instinct that kicks in.

In his book, John Huntsman says, *"Human seldom have created anything of lasting value unless they were tired or hurting."* What does this mean? It means that until there is adversity, things of lasting value will not be created. Another old adage says, *"Necessity is the mother of innovation."* I am convinced that when there is a great need for something, human beings will become innovative and creative. It is during times of crisis that life changes either positively or negatively. Imagine you are lying on your deathbed with three months to live. You have been diagnosed with a terminal disease according to the medical report.

What do you do? If it were I, I would pray a lot. I would repent and seek God's forgiveness. Crises will force you to pray if you have been taking prayer very lightly in your life. Imagine you have been a lazy worker at your organization and you are told that your position has been abolished? What do you do? You will start working hard to find another job. You will even begin to think of a vision and new direction for your life. It means you will change your lifestyle in innovative ways. If your house is being taken over by the bank because of mortgage. What do you? You will think of ways of getting another apartment or house.

Spiritual Growth

In the example of a terminal illness, I said there would be need for constant communion with God through prayer. Prayer is our decision to ask God for His intervention in our affairs on Earth.

When we pray, we are asking God for healing, direction, favor, mercy, forgiveness or provision. This process of prayer eventually makes us grow spiritually during moments of adversity. For example, David's faith and spiritual growth expanded because of the various tests and wars that he encountered. In addition, Abraham faith was strengthened because of the problems that he faced before God gave him a son.

Economic Growth

You will recall my explanation about Chinese ideas about a crisis. Every crisis has two sides - danger and opportunity. You can use adversity to benefit you by exploring new opportunities. New opportunities mean new businesses, starting your own company or organization, or new productive relationships.

Physical Growth

During times of adversity, your personal health will be impacted. The impact comes from psychological stress and trauma caused by crisis. Your blood pressure might go up. Your sleeping pattern might be altered. Your diet might also become affected. To ensure a good and healthy lifestyle, you will need to have regular physical exercises to keep your body and systems in shape and control. Regular exercises contribute to good life-balance and normality in mental health.

Mental Growth

Many people are frightened by crisis and they give up. In times of crisis, you need to feed your brain. You need new information, which comes from reading or studying and training. New information will help you have a different perspective of life. New knowledge comes from new information and the information could lead to transformation. What is my simple conclusion about growth in times of crisis? I believe all humans beings never grow in good times; instead, they grow in bad times. Crises will push you to grow. Your lifestyle will change. For example, Jesus became Jesus Christ after the crisis on the day of crucifixion. Peter became the rock and keeper of the flock after a crisis (John 21). David became a king after a crisis of fighting the Philistines and defeating Goliath. Among the world leaders that we have known, Nelson Mandela became the first black President of South Africa after surviving the jail sentence for 27 years. Ugandan leader, Yoweri Museveni, survived a crisis. Martin Luther King Jr became a global leader through the fight for racial equality and justice.

What crisis are you willing to go and come through? If you want to grow, get ready for crisis. You will never grow in good times. You will only grow in times of crisis. There is no growth without a crisis. There is no progress without opposition. There is no growth without pain. Pain will cause growth -No pain, no gain. It is up to you. You have a choice.

Tests of Maturity

How do we tell that a person or a leader is mature? How do we know that a believer of Jesus Christ is mature? Maturity is the only test that qualifies a person to lead. Your ability to lead will be tested when adversity strikes. Crisis is the true test of whether a person or a leader is mature, stable and strong. How a leader handles a crisis is the most important test of maturity. If you study the life of true Bible leaders, any one that you can recall, you will find that tests revealed their level of maturity. Any name that you call - Peter, David, Daniel, Meshach, or Paul - you will notice that all of these great leaders went through a crisis. Peter went through the crisis of denying His master Jesus Christ. David fought Goliath. Daniel was thrown in the lion's den. Meshach and his friends were thrown into the furnace. Paul was jailed several times.

All of those leaders went through difficult times in their leadership. What is common to all these leaders is that they were able to overcome. Overcoming a crisis is a product of maturity and faith. The more a leader gets tested by crisis, the more the leader grows stronger. There is complacency when everything seems to be okay and leaders never grow to become stronger in good times. The development and improvement in leadership is a result of attacks, pressure and crises. Crisis causes the leader's qualities to get refined and makes the leader utilize all hidden abilities to overcome a crisis.

True understanding of self and self-discovery are actualized in the moments of a crisis, . Crisis makes leaders thinkers, ideological, creative, innovative, and industrious. Leaders move to new realms because of crises, which is produced by creativity and innovation. A crisis is a source of all innovation when things are not working well. It forces innovation.

Belief Systems and Convictions

The leaders who emerge from a crisis are those that possess faith and convictions. A crisis will reveal the leader's beliefs as well as their deep convictions. What are your beliefs? What are your convictions? If you have been claiming that you believe in God, a crisis will reveal if that belief is true when adversity strikes. What do you do when a business that you have been depending on becomes bankrupt? Will you still believe that God is your provider? When you pass the test of crisis, then you are a true leader.

Crisis Causes Innovation

The Leader of the twelve disciples was one time in a crisis of feeding 5,000 men who followed him. The details of the story are presented here:

Sometime after this, Jesus crossed to the far shore of the Sea of Galilee (that is, the Sea of Tiberias), and a great crowd of people followed him because they saw the signs he had performed by healing the sick. Then Jesus went up on a mountainside and sat down with his disciples. The Jewish Passover Festival was near. When Jesus looked up and saw a great crowd coming toward him, he said to Philip, "Where shall we buy bread for these people to eat?" He asked this only to test him, for he already had in mind what he was going to do. Philip answered him, "It would take more than half a year's wages to buy enough bread for each one to have a bite! Another of his disciples, Andrew, Simon Peter's brother, spoke up, "Here is a boy with five small barley loaves and two small fish, but how far will they go among so many?" Jesus said, "Have the people sit down." There was plenty of grass in that place, and they sat down (about five thousand men were there). Jesus then took the loaves, gave thanks, and distributed to those who were seated as much as they wanted. He did the same with the fish. When they had all had enough to eat, he said to his disciples, "Gather the pieces that are left over.

Let nothing be wasted." So they gathered them and filled twelve baskets with the pieces of the five barley loaves left over by those who had eaten. After the people saw the sign Jesus performed, they began to say, "Surely this is the Prophet who is to come into the world." Jesus, knowing that they intended to come and make him king by force, withdrew again to a mountain by himself. (John 6:1-14)

The Critical Lessons from the Story

The above story is a clear manifestation of a crisis. Imagine 5,000 men gathered in one place. The crowd will be massive. I have worked with World Food Program, the United Nation's largest food distribution agency. It takes planning to have such a multitude of people to get food served without chaos and conflict. In the above story, we notice, Jesus asking where food can be acquired. Jesus innovatively believed God to multiply the available food of fish and bread. Jesus used the existing or available resources to overcome a crisis. The solution to problems created by a crisis depends on the leader's capacity to assess the existing resources. This takes innovation and creativity.

Further, organization is critical during a crisis. Leaders must take the challenge of organizing the followers. Jesus directed Philip to make the people sit down. In other words, Jesus told Philip to organize the people. Leaders are the organizers of followers during adversity.

What Does Innovation Mean?

Different scholars define innovation in their own ways. Here are mine:

- Ability to design new approaches to solve the emerging challenges from crises.
- Analysis of possibilities to deal effectively with crises using existing resources and capacities.
- Creation, development and application of techniques to solve new problems.
- Ability to think and design solutions of the problems that leaders face when a crisis hits.

No New Things on Earth

The Earth has existed for years from the time it was created. Millions of people have experienced or witnessed adversity. That means you are not alone. The current crisis that you are facing is not new. If it is conflict, there have been numerous conflicts around different countries the world over.

Consider floods, storms, hurricanes, or cyclones; all of these have occurred in the past and will continue to occur. No nation or president can stop those crises. King Solomon wrote in Ecclesiastes 1:9 that, "There is nothing new under the Sun." Solomon figured out that on Earth everything is old. There is nothing new on the planet.

Divorce is not new. Death is not new. Calamity due to loss of a spouse is not new. Losses of jobs have happened in the past and will continue to happen. The resources required for solving adversity are available on earth and people have solutions to those problems. Ideas on how to emerge with victory over a crisis are available. A new phone is an improvement over the existing phone. A latest vehicle is an improvement of the old model through creativity and innovation using new thinking, ideas and knowledge through application. Every person is created with the capacity to innovate but not everyone can think out of the box. Crisis requires out-of-the-box thinking.

Crisis Causes Creative Thinking

History is written when leaders overcome crisis. Overcoming a crisis will require creative or innovative thinking. Our brains kick into action when there is a crisis. Our brains start to think about the problem in order to solve it. There are several cases of creative or innovative thinking in the Bible. Moses, the leader of Israelites, was faced with a crisis to cross the Red Sea as the army of Egyptian Pharaohs approached them. Moses was in a desperate situation of saving the slaves and taking them to the Promised Land. Crossing the Red Sea was a crisis. There was no time for planning, meetings or mobilizing other leaders. There were no boats. There was no ferry. There were children, women and men both elderly and disabled. Probably only a few could swim. What did Moses do? He sought from God. God gave instructions on what to do. Exodus 14: 15-16 says, "Tell the Israelites to move on. Raise your staff and stretch out your hand over the see to divide the water so that the Israelites can go through the sea on dry ground." Reflect on this statement.

During times of crisis, examine the available resources. You never know if solution is available right there in front of you. Ask God for direction, guidance and instructions. Moses, together with the Israelites, were able to overcome the crisis. That example can apply to anyone facing his or her own "Red Sea". There are many examples of 'Red Seas' that we face every day, but always remember you are not alone. God is with you. Ask for guidance from God and close associates whom you trust. A crisis often reveals the need to use existing resources and capacities to overcome it innovatively. Times of crisis call for stability and not panic so that you can take advantage of opportunities and maximize the dividends of adversity. You only need to become an innovator and these crises will likely pass.

Further, crisis requires a change in the way things are done. There should be no more business as usual attitude. The old approaches and strategies are no longer being suitable for solving new problems. It requires changes in behavior, attitudes and thinking. It requires development of strategies and putting systems in place to get desired results or change goals to create a better and preferred future.

The impact of creative thinking is that new solutions will be designed. The whole nature of the crisis leads to innovation and creativity. A crisis also requires risk-taking. Risk-takers have the capacity to find opportunity and exploit those opportunities. It is worth noting that there will always be critics who attack your approaches to crises. There will be people who never agree with your strategies and systems. They will fight your efforts to discourage you.

Believe in Yourself

During moments of crisis, self-belief is critical for survival. It is the belief or faith that will carry you over and above crisis. Sometimes, God brings crises so we can trust Him. If you consider the story of "Daniel in the den of lions", it was faith that kept him alive. You know the story. How many lions are you about to face? How many obstacles are you facing? Another case study is the story of how Jesus dealt with the storm. The Biblical text is presented in the next passage. Doubt is the enemy of faith. Faith gives us the confidence that the future will be much better than the current circumstances. Self-belief is critical in times of unexpected change or rapid change.

Jesus Calms the Storm

One day Jesus said to his disciples, "Let us go over to the other side of the lake." So they got into a boat and set out. As they sailed, he fell asleep. A squall came down on the lake, so that the boat was being swamped, and they were in great danger. The disciples went and woke him, saying, "Master, Master, we're going to drown!" He got up and rebuked the wind and the raging waters; the storm subsided, and all was calm. "Where is your faith?" he asked his disciples. In fear and amazement, they asked one another, "Who is this? He commands even the winds and the water, and they obey him. (Luke 8: 22-25)

There was a crisis as the disciples were heading over to another location across the lake. Jesus who was a leader of the twelve fell asleep. However, as Jesus slept, the boat was under great waves. The whole team was in great danger. In the midst of this crisis, there was an outcry that the whole team was about to drown.

Jesus got up and rebuked the storms. The disciples were amazed at what happened when the storm subsided and calmed down. Let us examine how Jesus dealt with this crisis. Jesus asked a simple question: Where is your faith?

During a crisis, the need for faith is more important and must be applied for successful living. As in the case above, the leader must have the capacity to apply their faith during crisis. The final point I want to make here is that, without faith, a crisis will destroy the leaders and followers. There are times when leaders and followers need to act based on faith.

Crisis Produces Maturity and Completeness

When a crisis comes, it comes to make people mature and complete. The apostle James wrote a statement that changed my life about crises, trials and various challenges or test that come against you. What is maturity? What is completeness? Maturity is the capacity to face trials, challenges and tests of different kinds without losing joy and stability. Completeness is having a well-rounded character. Mature people therefore are able to share joy and enjoy sorrow.

Crisis is a Preparation Phase to Maturity

Any crisis that you overcome makes you stronger. It makes you mature. Consider the message from James:

Consider it pure joy, my brothers and sisters, whenever you face trials of many kinds, because you know that the testing of your faith produces perseverance. Let perseverance finish its work so that you may be mature and complete, not lacking anything. If any of you lacks wisdom, you should ask God, who gives generously to all without finding fault, and it will be given to you. But when you ask, you must believe and not doubt, because the one who doubts is like a wave of the sea, blown and tossed by the wind. That person should not expect to receive anything from the Lord. Such a person is double-minded and unstable in all they do. (James 1:2-4)

Crisis Leads to Character Formation and Transformation

Many people lose their character in times of crisis, yet crisis is supposed to make them have a strong character. Let us examine the concept of character: Character is a commitment and dedication to standards without wavering. Leaders who have strong character will be appointed to take up some offices without them being present during the selection or voting process.

How strong is your character? A strong character is needed especially in times of rapid change. It is essential in times of uncertainty or turbulent times. Followers of leaders need confidence from the leader. A leader whose character is weak will not only destroy the followers, but also impact on their destiny.

Chapter Eleven

TWELVE STEPS TO MANAGE CRISES

"I am a firm believer in the people. If given the truth, they can be depended upon to meet any national crisis. The great point is to bring them the real facts." **~ Abraham Lincoln**

How Do You Manage a Crisis That Has Affected You?

We have explored the meaning of a crisis. We have also identified the two types of crises that often attack individuals, families, communities, regions and nations or organizations. The several examples of crises have been presented for better understanding of the different types of crisis. The positive and negative impacts of crises have also been examined and discussed. I have worked with several organizations that deal with emergencies and crisis of the highest magnitudes. Through that experience and research, I have come to understand that the following steps are essential in helping one respond effectively to a crisis.

The purpose of presenting these steps is to offer direction so that the effects of a crisis are minimized and lives are saved or restored. A natural crisis always affects livelihoods, resources and impacts negatively on communities.

What Does It Mean "to Manage"?

The word manage has a connection to management. Management is a process of dealing with or controlling things or people. When things happen, you have to find ways of dealing with it. There are sometimes situations when things change or people change. You will need to be able to manage, deal with it or take control. Management also means the process of organization and coordination of activities to achieve pre-defined goals and objectives. To manage means to create policies, rules, guidelines, organize, plan, control, and direct all efforts and resources of the organization to achieve desired objectives and intended results and outcomes.

Twelve Steps For The Management Of Crises

Step One: Assess the Critical Needs

This is first and the most critical part of managing a crisis. A leader and those around must carry out an assessment of essential needs. The critical needs are those that are useful and relevant in crisis for saving lives. Critical needs are needs that are indispensable for human survival. The critical needs include food, water, shelter, security, safety, health and protection. Every person, when affected by a crisis, will have a need for critical needs to survive. How then do you carry out a needs assessment? Needs assessment is estimating what is required. Assessing needs involves collecting information about the needs that should be met or satisfied. In order to assess the needs, leaders must have their teams obtain answers to the assessment questions below. The following questions must be asked during needs assessment:

1. What do you need in order to survive during a crisis?
2. Where can you get what is necessary?
3. How can you obtain what is needed?
4. Why do you need to meet those needs?
5. What is the capacity of those affected by crisis to support themselves?
6. When can you get the needs?
7. Who needs assistance and who does not need assistance?
8. Where are those affected by a crisis?
9. Who can you work with to meet the needs identified?
10. Who are your partners?
11. What is the capacity of the partners?
12. What can the partners provide to meet the needs?
13. Who are the people who must be contacted and involved?

Step Two: Analyze Critical Needs

The second step that is critical is analyzing the needs and prioritizing which ones are urgent and important. The analysis involves asking the questions: Why, when, where, how and what. Let me explain this further. During analysis, a leader and followers decide and classify the needs. Some needs are urgent and important. Further, leaders also need to assess the critical or the lifesaving needs. The less critical needs must not be included in what is required. What do you need to survive? What are your physical, financial, healthy, social, economic or psychological needs? Analysis of needs allows you to determine what is necessary and essential. You also eliminate unnecessary wants, demands and non-lifesaving items on the list. At the end, you will get a priority list that gives you clear focus.

Step Three: Develop a Strategic Response Plan

The third step is developing a strategy and plan for response. A strategy is an action plan or a prepared policy that is used for achieving the primary goals. A strategy can also be considered as a master plan. A strategy can also be a gameplan. When a football team is losing during the first half of the game, the coach must come up with a revised gameplan. A gameplan is what the team must do to win the game with the next half. Consider the military during the war or battle time. Military leaders will have to develop and design a strategy for winning the war. A strategy is an art of planning as well as a way of directing the operations and movements of military troops to the enemy positions during the war or battle. The strategy is the tactics that must be adopted to achieve the goals for saving lives and reducing the impact of a crisis.

A strategy response plan will contain the following aspects:
1. Set the goals to be achieved.
2. Set the deadline to achieve each target.
3. Decide on what results you expect to gain.

4. Analyze the risks that will be encountered.
5. Decide on your planning assumptions.
6. Assess your strengths and weaknesses.
7. Determine how to measure when objectives have been achieved.
8. Analyze your environment and factors that will affect expected results.
9. Set the targets and benchmarks for measuring each goal or the goals.z

Step Four: **Set the Strategic Goals to be Achieved**

Setting strategic goals is an important action for you or the organization. The goals must be clear and smart. SMART goals are those that are simple, measurable, achievable, and realistic and timely. Do not set so many goals that can cause frustration and anxiety. Goals must help you to decide on what needs to be achieved. A minimum of four goals and a maximum of eight goals must be agreed. Do not set or agree on too many goals. Too many goals will always cause confusion, fear, and frustration. It is always important to set a small number of critical goals. You can have as many activities as possible but goals must be achieved.

Goals must be kept simple in order to be done. It must be noted that only quality goals must be stated and pursued. To realize a quality change, a quality choice must be pursued and done. A quality change is the one that will always lead to a permanent change and improvement. All other fake choices will bring another crisis and hence produce disaster.

The Characteristics of Good and Attainable Goals:

1. Goals must be simple.
2. Goals must be measurable. This is how to measure success. Set the indicators for each goal.
3. Goals must be achievable. Decide on a goal that you can achieve.
4. Goals must be realistic. Do not propose what is not easy to achieve.
5. Goals must be time bound. There must be a timeline for each goal.

Step Five: Carry Out the Agreed Activities

Goals cannot be achieved unless small steps are taken to accomplish the goals. For each goal, a set of activities must be agreed upon, decided and then implemented. The activities to be carried out must have a timeline set and decided. The people who will make the activities must be known and responsibilities must be assigned. An activity map or action plan must be prepared. Activities must be carried out systematically and consistently with commitment to achieve desired goals. It is like building a house; poor activities implementation will have long-term consequences on the building and occupants. People with capacity, skills, competence, knowledge and experience must be given the responsibility to implement or carry out activities. For instance, someone with limited knowledge on electrical works cannot be given tasks to carry out electrical works in a building. You must be mindful of who carries out the planned activities.

Action Plans Specifies the Following:

1. Who will do the activity to achieve the goal?
2. When will the activity be done?
3. For how long will the activity be conducted?
4. Where will the activity be implemented?
5. Who is responsible for the activity?
6. Review the action and assess which activities have been completed and which ones have not been completed.

Step Six: Identify the Potential Obstacles to Overcome

It is also critical that potential obstacles are identified. Obstacles are hindrances that can stop the implementation of agreed actions. Obstacles are hurdles and barriers that impact the implementation of the plans and attainment of goals. For each goal, it is critical to identify all the potential hindrances that are likely to block an individual, community, leaders or organization to achieve intended goals. Once the potential obstacles have been identified, determine how to overcome the obstacles. Obstacles, operational constraints and challenges must also be documented and projected. Plans to overcome those obstacles or barriers must also be put in place.

Examples of Obstacles:
1. Lack of money or funds.
2. Lack of knowledge and skills.
3. Lack of equipment and tools.
4. Conflicts.
5. Destroyed bridges.

6. Natural disasters (e.g., hurricanes, cyclones, typhoons, tsunamis, floods, storms).
7. Security restrictions.
8. Obstructions and distractions.
9. Competition from competitors or other stakeholders.
10. Poor relationships and partnerships.
11. Lack of qualified and right people, friends and workers.

Once the obstacles have been identified, they should be prioritized. Identify single barriers that affect the attainment of the set goals.

Step Seven: Monitor the Implementation of Activities

Another important step is monitoring how activities are being carried out to achieve the desired goals. For each goal and activity, monitoring must be conducted. A dedicated person must be assigned to monitor. To monitor means observing and checking the progress being made to achieve and accomplish the activities that contribute to the attainment of strategic goals. Monitoring also means the day-to-day function by leaders and managers to assess how the activities are being completed and results are being achieved.

Furthermore, monitoring is a daily activity where data is collected and analyzed to make correct decisions and solve any emerging problems affecting the attainment of desired goals. Monitoring is carried out from the start of the project until the completion of the project. Monitoring is a continuous activity and must be conducted consistently. Monitoring involves asking questions, which are related to efficiency, effectiveness, and relevance.

In other words, monitoring asks the following questions to achieve intended goals:

1. How efficient have you been?
2. How effective have you been?
3. Are the activities relevant?
4. Are the activities implemented related to the primary goals?

Step Eight: Review and Evaluate Plans

This step is related to the last step above. Reviewing and evaluating the strategies is critical in achieving goals that have been set in the strategy. For each goal, an evaluation must be carried out. Evaluation is a periodic activity that may be done by both insiders- and outsiders.

If it is done with internal staff, it is known as the review or internal evaluation. If done by outsiders, it is called an external evaluation. Reviewing is checking if what was planned has been accomplished and stating reasons for non-accomplishment.

What is the Purpose for Undertaking Evaluation?

1. Helps to assess the degree of efficiency.
2. Contributes to determine the level of effectiveness.
3. Determines the relevance.
4. Determines the achievement in impact.
5. Ensures sustainability is achieved.
6. Enables organizational learning.

Steps Nine: **Mobilize the Resources Required**

Another critical step is developing a plan to mobilize resources. Resource mobilization consists of all activities carried out to secure new as well as additional resources for achieving goals that have been established. Resource mobilization is the process of getting resources from the resource provider, using different mechanisms. The purpose of resource mobilization is acquiring resources to implement the organizations' work and to achieve pre-determined goals of the organization.

Resource Mobilization Involves:

1. Using existing resources to achieve set goals.
2. Maximizing the use of available resources.
3. Scanning to identify the source of resources.
4. Scanning for new opportunities.
5. Identifying resource gaps.
6. Submitting applications for grants or funds to donors.
7. Preparing work plans, budgets and projects.
8. Acquiring the needed resources in a timely and cost efficient manner.
9. Advocating for the right type of resource, at the right time, at the right price and making the right use of acquired resources.

10. Ensuring optimum utilization of resources received.

Why Must Resource Mobilization Be Undertaken?

The importance of resource mobilization includes:
1. Enables the organization continues to provide services to clients and stakeholders.
2. Supports the sustainability of the organization.

What is Meant by Sustainability?

Although sustainability is often identified as having sufficient funds to cover an organization's activities, it is a broader concept. There are three major streams of sustainability: institutional, financial and programmatic. Each is vital to the survival of an organization. The strategic plan is the anchor, or road map, in which an organization's programs, structure and systems, and financials for reviewing and identifying new business opportunities. These new directions or new business opportunities are then pursued using a clear resource mobilization strategy.

For organizations, resource mobilization strategy might include:
1. Writing proposals.
2. Submitting grant applications.
3. Drafting new business cases.
4. Producing business plans.

Steps Ten: Share and Manage Information
This is a big one. The sharing of information is very critical for teams, groups or organizations when there is a crisis. Information is vital for decision-making and taking corrective actions. Leaders, managers, and followers must continually share information.

Information can be shared through social networks, internet and reports. The management of information deals with the process of getting information from one or more sources, keeping the information, sharing information and discarding the information that does not add value. It is important to note that information must be carefully shared with stakeholders involved in crisis management.

Information Management is Important Because:
1. Information management gives managers and leaders knowledge.
2. Knowledge allows leaders and managers to take effective decisions.
3. Effective decisions lead to the making of appropriate actions.
4. Appropriate actions result in delivery of meaningful results.

Step Eleven: Coordinate Joint Action

The last step is coordinating with the teams and partners to make sure everything is conducted in a smooth and uniform way to achieve the goals. The purpose of joint action is to save lives. For an organization, for example, meeting times and coordination of activities must be known.

Joint action helps to:
- Ensure accountability and responsibility.
- Facilitate participation.
- Promote partnership.

- Agree on critical needs or priorities.
- Monitor progress.
- Mobilize resources.
- Develop the strategic plans.
- Agree on goals and indicators.
- Reduces confusion and crisis

Step Twelve: Develop a Recovery Plan

When the crisis has been managed, another plan must be produced to facilitate recovery and long-term development. A recovery plan will consist of goals, indicators, and targets. A similar process is followed from number one to number twelve. The difference is that during the recovery phase, the crisis has been managed and dealt with.

Chapter Twelve

DISCOVERING YOUR GIFT AND DIVINE ASSIGNMENT

"Everything passes. Joy. Pain. The moment of triumph; the sigh of despair. Nothing lasts forever - not even this." **~ Paul Stewart**

The Unemployment Crisis in the World

Unemployment is one of the greatest challenges of today's dynamic world. In every continent, there are thousands and millions of people who continually have to embrace the crisis of unemployment. Unemployment is a serious challenge. There are millions of people who are experiencing the effect of it. Although several countries believe that employment creation is the responsibility of the government in power, there needs to be a shift in this kind of thinking. I am convinced that the discovery of personal gift and divine assignment will make room or open doors for anyone in the world. That is why, for instance, great musicians, top politicians, businesses men or women, professional athletes and others hardly ever have to worry about employment. In the next pages, we shall be exploring the various concepts of job crises. We will dive into deeper insights and wisdom on the journey to self-discovery of your uniqueness and significance.

Job Crisis and Career Loss

There are millions of people who are employed in organizations (e.g., small, large, public, private, or even multinational). When you are employed, it means you do not own the organization or corporation. Your being in that organization, your remaining in it depends on your capacity to carry out the assigned duties to the satisfaction of your employer.

However, if the employer is satisfied with your performance, then you can keep being employed. If the employer is dissatisfied with your performance, then you might not keep that job for a very long time. Your failure to perform to the expectations of the employer or meet the expected performance standards will cause you to lose that job. You might be fired, laid off or downsized. When any of these events happen without your expectations, it will become a job crisis. That is, it is a circumstance or an event that happens without you being aware it is coming. It can cause stress, regret, and fear, health problems such as high blood pressure, hopelessness, despair or even suicide.

Sometimes, a job crisis is caused by introduction of new technologies in the job market or hiring of cheap labor. There are companies or organizations in the world that no longer employ many people (e.g., Google, Amazon, etc.). These companies operate digital businesses. The need for employees has been eliminated by laborsaving approaches and technologies. Besides, there are millions of prospective employees who have all kinds of degrees or qualifications but are still unemployed. These people are qualified but are unable to find stable and well-paying jobs. Some people experience a job crisis because they have no skills that are required or needed by the world.

The loss of a job might result into the end of your career. A career is something treasured by most people. When you lose a career that you have labored to keep for over a decade or more, you might be forced to start over again. Where do you start? What is it that you will do that will make you happy and effective? There must be some ideas, dreams or plans that you have been putting on hold. What should you do then?

Entrepreneurship Mindset

In times of crisis, you will find people starting side businesses or income- generating activities. The people who can start their own small enterprises can end up becoming self-employed and owners of large business. However, entrepreneurship is not as easy as it sounds. I have been a victim of mismanagement of an enterprise. I started a bakery business in Uganda when I was working in Somalia. The business was for my young relatives with college degrees to have a start-up job. Do you know what happened after investing over $40,000? The business collapsed. It failed. We had a good start. We had good products. We had a clientele base. We had resources, equipment and transport facilities. We had a brand name, "Daily Choice Bread". We had all that was required to become successful. We had a registered company. We had packaging materials. But what happened? There was gross mismanagement. To succeed as an entrepreneur, you will need to be knowledgeable about effective management. Effective management is your safeguard from closing down a good business or losing resources. Crises will test your ability to manage. Crises will test your effective management capacity.

Divine Assignment and Responsibility

On planet earth, there are millions of people who have been oppressed by circumstances such as poverty, fear, and environmental factors. They have been "beaten down" by life. People take responsibility for their decisions, choices, and actions. The children may blame their parents for their predicaments or current circumstances. The slaves blame their masters. The students blame teachers. Citizens blame their leaders and governments. The blacks blame the whites and so forth. They are perplexed by the complexities of life. They are left wondering what do with the uncertain future, and rapid and changing world. They are not aware of how to make changes in their own lives let alone their organizations.

All the "blame games" and behaviors started in Genesis 3 during the fall of man. Adam blamed Eve. Eve blamed the serpent. God who is Holy and keeps his holy word does not like or accept "blame games". He is holy, which means He is "One." "One", on the other hand, means "integrated." "Integrated" is a root word for "integrity." Integrity then means "One." God does not change. He is the same, yesterday, today and forever. God gives laws and promises. The reason we as humans trust God is that His nature, image and character are unchanging. Violation of laws, has consequences.

God desires his creatures to be responsible. Being responsible means you can respond to your circumstances, challenges and situations. God created humans with what I call the most powerful force, will. Humans are not like animals who operate on instinct. We are creatures who operate and act based on will and power of choice. Our choices and will decide where life will take us. You can decide today, tomorrow or next year to do something different, and your life will be different. Our choices and decisions make us different from one another.

Before we dive into discovering your gift and divine assignment, I want to draw your attention to how to protect your future. I am sharing these deep secrets, and I believe they will be of great help to anyone who reads and masters these concepts.

Here are the basic statements for you to master:

1. **Life is a gift and privilege.**
   It is not a plague and therefore must be handled with great care and reverence.

2. **There is no future for anyone who is unfaithful**.
   If you are faithless and not committed in life to a cause, you will lose your future.

3. **Bad environments destroy good destinies in life.**
   You need to monitor whom you associate and relate with consistently. Otherwise, your God-chosen destiny will be truncated.

4. A quality choice makes a permanent change in areas of life.

Check your personal choices in life.

5. Decisions determine our destinies in life.

Where we end up in life is a matter of our decisions. Why? We are the total of all the decisions we have made up to this point in time.

What does it mean by the concept of a divine assignment? I do not know what you believe about God. As for me, I believe that God created everything that is seen and unseen, visible or invisible, including me. God creates things for a reason. God creates things to accomplish a defined assignment. That assignment is what I call a "Divine assignment." When you study the scriptures, you will find many examples of leaders who were at first employed, but later in their lives decided to carry out their divine assignments.

A divine assignment is your God-given purpose in life, something that God created you to accomplish. God created all things to accomplish a certain purpose on earth. Nothing is created without a reason. Nobody can do what you were created to do on earth. Consider the job you are doing. Anybody with the same training can be employed or hired to carry out your responsibilities and duties.

However, with your divine assignment, no person can do it except you. You are created to carry out your divine assignment. Let us look at a few examples. Simon Peter, for example, had a job or a career in fishing. His divine assignment however, was leading the church organization when Jesus Christ left to go back to Heaven where he came from after completing His assignment of redeeming and reconciling you back to God. David is another example. David was the son of Jesse and a shepherd boy. God prepared him to lead the Israelites and establish the city of Jerusalem. Paul, on the other hand, was trained as a lawyer. God, however, called him to be an apostle, a preacher, author and a teacher. He wrote most of the books in New Testament.

In your place of divine assignment, no man can fire or terminate your appointment. Only God can fire or terminate you. Do you remember Saul who was the first king of Israel who was fired from the position because of disobedience to God's instructions? Your assignment is manifested in gifts, talents, visions, wishes, ideas, dreams and problems that require you to solve.

However, many times we never take time to consider these things. For instance, when God gives you a vision, you have to write it down, (Habakkuk 4:6) and you have to develop a plan of action (Proverbs 16). Without a plan, it is impossible to achieve a vision. Gifts are also revealed in passions and recurrent ideas (Proverbs 12:5).

Think about the things that you are passionate about. Write them down and do them. Think about what you wish you were doing. Write them down and do them. Give it all your best. When you pursue them with all your heart, you become the person God intended you to become. You will be at peace with yourself, and you will not be intimidated or afraid of anything.

The process of gift discovery involves the following steps:
1. Finding the gift.
2. Defining the gift.
3. Refining the gift.
4. Distributing the gift through serving others.
5. Serving your gift. A gift makes you a slave, not of people, but of your gift.
6. Committing to your gift. To be great you have to be a total slave of your gift. You have to be dedicated, loyal, and sacrifice.

As I conclude, you might discover your gift, but if you violate God's laws, you will have to pay a great price and suffer the consequences. I have met many people who think they are smart. They can play with laws but their future will likely be truncated. God's words say the wages of sin is death. Let me put it this way, violation of God's laws attracts consequences. You become fruitless instead of becoming fruitful. Be fruitful by abiding in God. (John 15)

Jobs

When you go to college, you will be trained in a particular field based on a given curriculum. That curriculum produces people who have the same knowledge, attitudes, experience, and skills. If you can perform a job, then another person can also perform the job that you have. Take, for example, the teaching profession. If you are trained as a teacher, then you can teach. The difference might be in communication abilities, styles or presentations but the bottom line is that a teacher can always teach. Suppose you have been trained as a nurse, then any other similarly trained individual can do your job of nursing.

However, if you have specialized skills, then nobody can do your job. Do you see the difference? If you can be replaced easily then that is a job. If it had to have a replacement of you, then that is a divine assignment. It is important to note that a job is always temporary. A job might be your career. You can be forced to leave your career.

However, the beauty of a divine assignment is that you do it for the rest of your life. Jesus Christ discovered his divine assignment even though he worked briefly with his parents in a carpentry workshop. Look at other examples of people who discovered their gifts and divine assignment. Mother Teresa was simple teacher who inspired millions to serve the needy and poor people of India.

Consider Nelson Mandela who was trained as a lawyer but found his assignment in the fight for freedom from apartheid. He was born as a freedom fighter. His assignment was to fight freedom, justice and equality. My question to you: Do you know yourself? Have you discovered what you were created to do? What are you passionate about doing? What are your gifts? What can you do?

Divine Assignments, Jobs and Careers

Do not get me wrong on the issues about careers. Careers are all good things. They are helpful and help us prepare for a divine assignment. Every job that I have held was a preparation for my divine assignment. I have always known that I will never hold a job for all my lifetime. I might one day be laid off or lose a contract. I could be fired.

Nevertheless, what I have always done is to prepare myself for my divine assignment so that I can use my God-given and unique gifts. No person can be like me ever on earth because I have discovered my gifts. Do you have knowledge of your gift? When I discovered my gifts, I became very confident and fearless. I know you might be scared of your future; it is because you have no idea of your gifts, your talents, abilities, passions or maybe even your dreams.

I decided years back in my job to invest heavily on my gifts. I believed that in the future, people would pay me for my gifts. Every single day, I keep looking at my dreams and gifts. I keep investing in my gift. I keep refining my gifts. I am preparing to deploy my gifts to the world to make it benefit humanity. What are you currently doing to develop your gifts? Are you practicing? Or are you expecting your life to become better just by doing nothing?

Do you remember the life of David? He was the youngest son of Jesse. His job was taking care of the flock of his father or shepherding the sheep. During the time that he was busy taking care of the flock, he mastered and learned how to engage with lions and bears. He learned how to swing the sling. He gained a lot of experience. His skills helped him save the flock from the lions and bears. As a matter of fact, he killed a bear and lion at one time while on the job.

All these experiences, however, were a preparation for a divine assignment. David killed Goliath and defeated the enemies of Israel. The job that David was doing prepared him for his eternal assignment. David was being prepared to lead, be courageous, strong, fearless and confident. David was aware that if he could kill a lion, then he could fight the enemies of Israel. He was never afraid. He knew his gift and divine assignment. If you have knowledge of your assignment, you cannot be intimidated by anyone.

I recall when I was 15 years old and my mother had just passed on. I was staying with my siblings and cousins. We were all young at that time. There was war going on in our home district and other parts of country. I recall always advising my relatives about how they need to keep away from relationship especially those involving girls. I did not know at the time I was doing what I was created to do. I was saving my sisters from the deadly HIV/AIDS epidemic. The HIV/AIDS killed several people but none of us acquired the virus that causes AIDS. Later on in life, when I started to think about my life's purpose, I concluded that I was born to save lives and help other people. I have worked in large humanitarian organizations whose mission has been the same as my own - to save lives and empower people as leaders. Many people are inspired by what I write or speak. It brings life to those that hear me. Can you imagine?

Distinction of a Job from a Divine Assignment

1. Every job is temporary but your divine assignment is to do the work God created you to do. It is the work you are born to do. A job is temporary but a divine assignment is permanent.
2. You receive training for jobs. Your divine assignment may not require much training.
3. A job requires a certain level of skills. Your divine assignment requires using your gifts.
4. An employee with a job can be fired. For your divine assignment, you cannot be fired.
5. Every job has a requirement to retire. Your divine assignment does not require retirement only finishing.

Jobs Combined with Your Divine Assignment

A job and divine assignment are related. A job might prepare you for a divine assignment. Every job that you have may be used to develop your gifts so that you can serve the gifts to the world. You also might use a job to continue refining your gift. I have had many jobs but I used the jobs to continue to improve on my gifts. When a job ends, you will still have your gifts with you. Nobody takes away your gifts. However, a job can be taken away.

Do you remember the story of Moses? Moses was working as a shepherd with his father-in-law Jethro. God had given Moses leadership gifts while working there. When his job was over, he took over to be a leader. Moses lived in the Midian Desert. How did being a shepherd prepare Moses to be a leader? The job gave him skills that were also needed in leading people. He needed to know how to handle people with patience he showed in taking care of sheep. Further, the job gave him experience of desert conditions. Moses worked for years. He learned how to organize the sheep. He also had to learn how to lead and guide reluctant followers. In addition, he also had to learn how to get water and pasture for the sheep. Later on, Moses would have to find water for the people in the same desert. The job equipped and prepared him for his divine assignment. What was it? I believe Moses was born to provide leadership and set the oppressed people free from slavery.

When I was 15 years old, I was always helping my grandmother to do some tasks. I discovered that I was created for a reason to help others and teach them. As grew, I noted that I have a special gift of teaching. Everyone whom I have met will tell you about my gift. All I have been doing is developing my gift so I can lead in an area of my gift. As I work, I am also developing my gift and divine assignment. As I studied my personal life, I realized my inherent gifts and I have continued to put a lot of effort to develop them. I have seen how people are attracted to me because of my gift. I used to have a misleading idea that people loved me for no reason, but I came to understand after several disappointments that people come to me because of my gift. I decided that I would love myself more. In spite of that, I will still serve with my gift.

Joseph the Dream Interpreter

Genesis 41 gives an account of the events of Joseph's life. It is a fascinating story. He was the youngest of the children of his father, Jacob. Joseph had a gift of dreams. He had two dreams that he shared with his family. As a result of sharing the dream, he was hated by his own brothers. They treated him terribly. They tore his clothes. They threw him in a pit. They sold him to Egyptian traders. He was later taken to prison. A woman lied against him and accused him of wanting to rape her. At the end, he still came out of prison. He interpreted Pharaoh's dream. He was appointed to manage the humanitarian crisis. What was Joseph's divine assignment? He was created to save the lives of families from dying from the famine that hit all the land of Egypt.

If Joseph had not been created, probably all his family would have perished of starvation and famine. What is your assignment? Remember, your knowledge of your assignment and fulfillment of that assignment will require some form of testing. When you start to speak about that assignment, you will go through your own "desert", storms, problems, obstacles and chaos. On the other hand, if it is from God and not concoction, you will achieve it.

The Power of Carrying Out a Divine Assignment

Can you imagine the power of your assignment? I believe the greatest power of a divine assignment is that it will always protect you from a job crisis. When you know your assignment, you will always have confidence. You will have courage. You are convicted about it. You are motivated to carry it on. You see no obstacles. Instead, you see opportunities. You become focused. You become disciplined. You know what people will be looking for. You will never be discouraged. Perhaps you have been wondering about your life. Your life is like a seed. A seed can be lying dormant but it still has gifts. If the seed brings forth its gifts, people will be attracted to it. Your life is the same way. Do not continue wondering about your gift or assignment. You need to think about it and initiate action.

I recall that one day I had a meeting with a close friend of mine in a hotel in Kampala. We had not met for several months because I was always out of the country. He said, "If my hands and head is chopped off, then I will be finished but as long I have the two; I have my "gift". This friend has always sought advice from me in many areas of his life. My interpretation of what my friend statement is that nobody can take away your gifts. You have the gifts that no other person on earth have. You are unique. You are special. Those gifts make you significant and valuable. Therefore, your future is trapped in your gift, the seed that you have not planted. You need to take chances and tap into your gift.

Furthermore, the people who carry out jobs also make a difference. They create impacts. The people who pursues their divine assignment will always leave a huge impact and a difference. Look at Moses; he left an impact of freeing the slaves from the oppression from Pharaoh. Apostle Paul is credited for writing letters to different churches. He wrote to the Romans, Thessalonians, Ephesus, Corinthians and other young leaders such as Timothy, etc. What are you known for? What will people remember about you? What gifts will people come to get from you?

THE MESSAGE TO THE CURRENT AND FUTURE LEADERS

"Some of the greatest battles will be fought within the silent chambers of your own soul."
~ Ezra Taft Benson

As a Leader, So What?

As a leader of the family, community, church, corporation, organization or even a nation, there are some critical decisions that must be made to prepare for crises. Crisis is going to be "part and parcel" of life. Crises will affect the politics of a nation. It will affect the environment, society or community. It will affect the people, including the unborn. Crisis requires that leaders must themselves become overcomers. They must also prepare their people as overcomers. Preparation requires knowledge of how to deal, overcome and manage crises.

The world has continued to witness one crisis to another. Everyday things continue to get worse than yesterday. The problems of terror will continue and the strategies used to cause crises will get complicated. In order to survive and thrive, there will be need for knowledge, wisdom and application of principles. Those perspectives have been laid down in this book for your use. You must know that everybody will experience a crisis at some point in his or her. It is certain. As you emerge out of one crisis, another will be waiting to attack you. You might experience one crisis in January followed by another crisis in June and July or from one year to another. You need to get prepared.

Nobody is immune to a crisis. Everyone will experience it. Whether you believe in God or not. Whether you are a Christian, Hindu, Muslim or none of these religious groups. Whether you live in Africa or America. Whether you live in Europe or China. You will be affected by a crisis. Even those who are genuine Christians and believers in God will be affected. Crises will affect poor and even rich nations alike. Terror will happen in London just as it will happen in Paris, Brussels, Nairobi, Cairo or any tiny village in Somalia. Crises will be part of the equation of our life on earth. The big question is how you are going to deal, overcome and manage the next crisis that will hit you as a leader, family or nation. You will need a combination of strategies, approaches, principles and ideas. I appreciate you for reading my ideas on these issues.

How will you rise above all the challenges of crises? I have exposed the concepts that will be valuable for that purpose. You can contact the author for more training and preparation on how to deal, manage or overcome any crisis. I am available to help you, your organization or nation. My contact is available on page 208.

SALVATION PRAYER

This prayer is for you to receive Jesus Christ as your personal Lord and Savior:

Dear Heavenly Father and God of All Creation: You created and manufactured my life for a purpose, and without any mistake, I am aware that you created me to perform and fulfill my purpose and you desire that in me. I know that I have fallen and disobeyed your laws and principles, and now I have lost my sense of direction and purpose in life.

I am also aware that your Son Jesus Christ is the way, the truth, and life, and without Him, I can do nothing. I believe that with Him, I will discover my purpose. I, therefore, ask you in the Name of Jesus to cleanse my life and send your Holy Spirit to dwell in my life and heart to reveal my purpose and fulfill it and live effectively. I surrender to Jesus Christ as my personal Savior and My Lord, and I commit 100% to do your will and fulfill my purpose that you created me to finish. In the name of Jesus Christ, I have prayed, Amen.

If you sincerely prayed that prayer, please write to me using the address below and share your commitment with me. If you need more teachings on these secrets and principles, you can also write to me, and we can arrange and support you, your family, church, company or organization.

We offer training, coaching, mentoring, seminars and workshops to help people live effectively and show them how to apply these principles. In case you or your organization is interested in more training and empowerment, please send a message through the following means:

Dr. Samuel Odeke, DSL
C/O GILBD and CTSL Uganda
P.O. Box 34820 Kampala, Uganda
Or P.O. Box 2648 Mbale, Uganda
Telephone: +256783563417/782276765
E-mail: samuel.odeke@yahoo.com
Website: www.samuelodeke.com

ABOUT THE AUTHOR

Dr. Samuel Odeke earned a Doctorate of Strategic Leadership with specialization in Strategic Leadership from Regent University in 2017. He received an M.A in Organizational Leadership and Management from Uganda Christian University. He also holds a Post Graduate Diploma in Public Administration and Management and Masters of Management with Specialization in Public Administration and Management from Uganda Management Institute. Earlier, he received a Bachelor of Science Degree and Post Graduate Diploma in Education from Makerere University.

Dr. Odeke serves in various capacities such as an international civil servant, humanitarian worker, speaker, teacher, educator, leadership and management mentor and consultants for both private and public organizations. He travels to different countries annually, attends and facilitates international conferences, seminars, and workshops. To him leadership and management are two critical areas that need to be addressed if humanity is to achieve its purpose in life and release their potential. World problems are a result of bad leadership and poor management.

Dr. Odeke has worked with large humanitarian and development organizations among others such as World Vision, United Nations World Food Programme (WFP) and United Nations Children's Fund (UNICEF) among others. He has travelled in different countries such as Kenya, Rwanda, South Africa, Nigeria, Belgium, Spain, Netherlands, and the United States. Dr. Odeke believes that leadership can be developed through empowering, coaching and mentoring. He is a member of International Leaders Association (ILA), The Christian Book Sellers Association (CBA) and Africa Strategic Leadership Forum (ASLF).

Dr. Odeke had a very humble background is married with children. He experienced tragedy when he lost his mother at age 14, his grandfather at 15, and grandmother at 18. Those traumatic experiences changed his perception of life. As a result, he began to search for answers related to life. As a teenager, Dr. Odeke also witnessed the impact of war, conflict and massive cattle raids in his district of Bukedea (formerly part of Kumi district) in the late 1980s, where hundreds of lives and properties were lost. He survived death from both government soldiers and rebels.

Dr. Odeke, has applied the strategies in this book, since he was a teenager after the mother's early death, took the burden to support his siblings, it is also a story of great hardships, challenges, setbacks and crisis, but above all of vision, purpose and determination, of sorrow, success and triumph. Dr. Odeke is a real testimony of humble beginnings and God's divine power. He travels and passionately shares strategies for overcoming crisis.

REFERENCES

China Population 1950-2017. China population accessed from http://www.tradingeconomics.com/china/population on 29 October 2017

https://en.wikipedia.org/wiki/*Mary_Ka*y accessed on 21 April 2017.

Huntsman, J. (2005). *Winners Never Cheat*: Everyday Values We Learned as Children (but May Have Forgotten). Prentice Hall Professional.

Kay, M. (From Wikipedia): The free encyclopedia accessed from https://en.wikipedia.org/wiki/Mary_Kay accessed on 30 October 2017

Nevado, R. (2008): *Obama's comments of economic crisis*; accessed from http://www.realclearpolitics.com/articles/2008/09/obamas_remarks_on_the_economic.html#ixzz4e5fZc6JI